PROCEED AND
BE BOLD

PROCEED AND BE BOLD

Rural Studio After Samuel Mockbee

text by ANDREA OPPENHEIMER DEAN   photographs by TIMOTHY HURSLEY

Princeton Architectural Press, New York

Published by
Princeton Architectural Press
37 East Seventh Street
New York, New York 10003

For a free catalog of books, call 1.800.722.6657.
Visit our web site at www.papress.com.

All photographs © Timothy Hursley unless otherwise
indicated
Jennifer Bonner: 168–171
Samuel Mockbee, courtesy Jackie Mockbee and family:
11, 160, 162
Courtesy Rural Studio: 163, 164
Patrick McFarlin: 172
William Christenberry: 86, 87

Frontispiece and endpiece: Under a big tent, members
of Rural Studio plan out the Sub Rosa Pantheon, a
project based on drawings by Samuel Mockbee.

Library of Congress Cataloging-in-Publication Data
Dean, Andrea Oppenheimer.
  Proceed and be bold : Rural Studio after Samuel
Mockbee / text by Andrea Oppenheimer Dean ;
photographs by Timothy Hursley.
    p. cm.
  ISBN 1-56898-500-2 (alk. paper)
  1. Auburn University. Dept. of Architecture. Rural
Studio. 2. Architecture—Study and teaching—
Alabama—Hale County. 3. Vernacular architecture—
Alabama—Case studies. 4. Sustainable
architecture—Alabama—Case studies. 5. Poor—
Housing—Alabama. 6. Mockbee, Samuel—Influence.
I. Hursley, Timothy, 1955- II. Title.
  NA2300.A9D427 2005
  728'.1'09761—dc22
                          2004017680

Editing: Clare Jacobson
Design: Jan Haux

Special thanks to: Nettie Aljian, Nicola Bednarek, Janet
Behning, Megan Carey, Penny (Yuen Pik) Chu, Russell
Fernandez, John King, Mark Lamster, Nancy Eklund
Later, Linda Lee, John McGill, Katharine Myers, Jane
Sheinman, Scott Tennent, Jennifer Thompson, Joseph
Weston, and Deb Wood of Princeton Architectural Press
—Kevin C. Lippert, publisher

CONTENTS

6   Introduction

18   RURAL STUDIO REACTS TO ITS LOSS

20   Lucy's House

40   Shiles House

46   Antioch Baptist Church

54   UNDER ANDREW FREEAR, THE PACE INTENSIFIES

56   HERO Storefront

62   Akron Senior Center

68   Perry Lakes Park Pavilion

76   Room for Essie and Jab

82   PERSONALIZED PROJECTS BOTH BIG AND SMALL

84   Red Barn

92   Music Man's House

104 Perry Lakes Park Facilities

114 Newbern Little League Baseball Field

124 Thomaston Rural Heritage Center

132 EVER-CHANGING, THE RURAL STUDIO REMAINS A MOVING TARGET

134 Avery Organic Vegetable Stand

140 Ola Mae's Porch

146 Utility Now! Bicycle Street Sweepers

150 Bodark Amphitheater

152 Patrick House

160 Experiencing the Rural Studio:
     Interviews with Students, a Teacher, and a Client

168 Building a Pavilion
     Jennifer Bonner

172 Another Dimension of Sambo
     Jackie Mockbee

174 Project Credits

INTRODUCTION

THE RURAL STUDIO in southwest Alabama has been called "Redneck Taliesin," but the comparison is superficial. True, Samuel Mockbee and Frank Lloyd Wright, both founders of famed design/build programs, were charismatic teachers who pried open the minds of their students with evocative stories and practical lessons instead of dry theory. Wright spoke of Taliesin as having "simply shaken itself out of my sleeve." Mockbee's told his Rural Studio students, "Screw the theory; choose the more beautiful." But Wright, a surpassing egotist, saw himself as the embodiment of the Welsh magician and bard Taliesin and gathered apprentices in rural Wisconsin for his own greater good. Mockbee, humble and unassuming, wanted to do good for others. Wright was domineering, while Mockbee applied a light touch, cautioning students that goodness was more important than greatness, compassion more essential than passion. Wright was the elegant, autocratic Mr. Wright. Mockbee was an egalitarian and a populist who preferred being called "Sambo." You would find the bearish, bearded, sixth-generation Mississippian driving around Hale County, the Rural Studio's home, in a beat-up red pickup, wearing old clothes and an Auburn University baseball cap. He viewed himself as an iconoclast and a subversive. The same, of course, was true of Wright.

At the beginning of the 1990s, during a period of economic expansion for America's upper-middle and wealthy classes, Mockbee planted Auburn University's Rural Studio in Alabama's second poorest county, Hale. It is a place of hollows and flat fields that occasionally fold into rolling hills, a place of kudzu-shrouded trees and catfish farms. Underfoot, rust-red soil turns to dust under a blistering summer sun and to mud when it rains. Mockbee loved Hale's winding Black Warrior River, with its banks of dense piney woods, and its spectral buildings—frail, antebellum mansions and collapsing, weather-beaten barns, outbuildings, and warehouses—that speak of a prosperous agrarian past. He was drawn to Hale County in part because it is so poor. A place where thirty-five percent of the population lives in poverty obviously needed help and would force students to test their abstract notions about poverty by "crossing over into that other world, smelling it, feeling it, experiencing it," he said.

Mockbee also liked Hale County's isolation. Newbern, the one-store hamlet that is the Rural Studio's base, is 150 miles

The late Samuel Mockbee (seated near center) with Rural Studio students

from the university, 10 miles from the nearest eatery, and 45 miles from the closest movie house. Seclusion, combined with Mockbee's prohibition on television, concentrated students' minds on their building projects. At the Rural Studio they were exposed to the region's architectural history, read its literary giants, and absorbed Mockbee's lectures on responsibility and ethics. After hours, they shot the breeze late into the night.

Mockbee, who founded the studio with Auburn professor D. K. Ruth in 1992 and directed it until his death from leukemia in late 2001, was convinced that "everyone, rich or poor, deserves a shelter for the soul." He believed that architects should take the lead in procuring social and environmental change, but that they had lost their moral compass and become "house pets to the rich." The profession needed reform, he thought, and education was the place to start. "If architecture is going to nudge, cajole, and inspire a community to challenge the status quo into making responsible changes," he said, "it will take the subversive leadership of academics and practitioners who keep reminding students of the profession's responsibilities." He wanted to get students out of classrooms, usually dominated

The Rural Studio's first house has walls made of hay bales. Its adjacent smokehouse is of stones and colored glass.

by abstract drawing projects and solipsistic architectural theorizing, and into what he called "the classroom of the community." Under his direction, the Rural Studio brought fifteen or so second-year students to Hale County each semester to help design and build a house. A few fifth-year students stayed for a year to work on a community building, their thesis project. During Mockbee's last two years, the studio launched an outreach program, accepting a handful of students from other universities and other disciplines to undertake a variety of design and social work assignments.

The Rural Studio represents a vision of architecture that embraces not only practical architectural education and social welfare but also the use of salvaged, recycled, and curious materials to create an appreciation of place. "I want to be over the edge, environmentally, aesthetically, and technically," Mockbee said. His students used hay bales to build walls for the studio's first house. They employed worn-out tires for the walls of a chapel, discarded Chevy Caprice windshields for the roof of a community center, waste corrugated cardboard for a one-room dwelling, and surplus carpet tiles for a family home.

Transmuting ordinary materials into extraordinary objects, the studio's early buildings were obvious relatives of those Mockbee designed for his own clients. He described his architecture as contemporary modernism grounded in Southern culture, and found inspiration in such vernacular

sources as overhanging galvanized roofs, rusting metal trailers, dogtrot forms, and porches. His designs logically tended toward asymmetry and idiosyncrasy. "I'm drawn to anything that has a quirkiness to it, a mystery to it," he told me.

In 1998, Mockbee won the National Building Museum's first Apgar Award for Excellence; in 2000, he won a MacArthur "genius" grant; and in 2004, the American Institute of Architects honored him posthumously with their ultimate accolade, the AIA Gold Medal—less, presumably, for a body of built work than for translating convictions about ethical architecture into a successful educational and social program. Mockbee thought of the Rural Studio, in its ultimate distillation, as "about being decent and trying to provide a decent community for all citizens. Isn't working like this what architecture students should be doing?"

The influence of the Rural Studio is hard to quantify. Daniel Friedman, dean of the University of Illinois at Chicago's architecture program, says it has changed architectural education. William J. Carpenter, author of *Learning by Building*, observes that in 1992 there were eight or ten university-based design/build programs, while today there are thirty or forty. He says, "A lot of the increase had to do with Sambo." The charismatic Mockbee and his Rural Studio were featured on network television, including *CBS This Morning*, and in numerous national magazines. "It was the first time the public was captivated by an architectural model," Carpenter says. Another influence, he says, is graduates—about 450 by now. Many become purveyors of the Rural Studio's approach.

Although Frank Lloyd Wright's Taliesin carries on, much of its creativity and vitality died with its founder. Could the love child of Sambo Mockbee's imagination and convictions survive his death? If it did, could it escape being a weak sister to the original?

I am pleased to report that the Rural Studio thrives, a tribute to Mockbee's ideas. The studio is not quite the same and is not without criticism, even from within. But Mockbee understood change and welcomed it. He created the studio as a moving target. "I suspect Sambo would just think it was different and regret not being there," David Buege, a professor of architecture at Mississippi State University and a friend of Mockbee, told me.

Who is Andrew Freear?

There was never a doubt about who should succeed Mockbee. At the time of his death, the Rural Studio had two instructors. Steve Hoffman, the second-year instructor, was only twenty-six—"a wise baby," Mockbee called him. Hoffman did not consider himself a potential successor. Andrew Freear, thirty-four in 2001, instructed fifth year. Freear is a native of Yorkshire, England, and a product of London's Architectural Association. From 1994 until 1998, he lived in Chicago, working for local firms while teaching at the University of Illinois, Chicago. He signed on to teach at Auburn for the academic year 1998–99, and that is when he met Mockbee. "Sambo was nervous about hiring me," Freear says, "because I was an outsider, and he was afraid I'd be one of those three-days-a-week teachers who'd want to fix a program that wasn't broken."

Soon after arriving at the studio in 2000, Freear proved to be an around-the-clock teacher with a disciplined focus on projects and a tendency to sit back, watch, listen, and learn about his new locale. "Sambo and I were good together," he says. "I was a sort of utilitarian socialist and he was the artist who said, 'make it pretty.' That was refreshing, because most teachers want to theorize about this or that for four hours, and Sambo would just say, 'This is more beautiful than that.'"

Andrew Freear oversees a graduation ceremony.

Freear gained Mockbee's respect, and they became good friends, living together in a converted farmhouse when Mockbee was in Newbern. Toward the end of his life Mockbee began reducing his involvement in the studio—"backing away" is the way his widow, Jackie, puts it. "He knew it could stand on its own. But when Sambo died, I was scared to death, because you couldn't just hire someone else and put them out there." Freear was the obvious successor—the only person, really, who could take over. The studio formed ranks behind him, and Freear picked up the pieces and carried on, adopting one of Mockbee's slogans, "proceed and be bold." In 2002, Auburn appointed Freear co-director with Bruce Lindsey, head of Auburn's school of architecture. Mockbee was the heart and soul of the Rural Studio. His successor, though its most dominant presence and its public face, is not yet its spiritual center. That role may be held by the studio's founder in perpetuity.

The changes that have taken place under Freear's watch reflect, in part, his undivided focus on the studio and his fifth-year students. Mockbee spent weekends with his family in Canton, Mississippi, and increasingly channeled his waning energies into painting and design work. Freear lives at the studio full-time and is single. "Because Sambo was here part-time," he says, "his mode of operation—a result of his self-confidence, age, and experience—was to come in and know when to pat people on the back and give them a hug and just let them go with it." Freear says the studio misses "Sambo's light touch. My style is to be much more involved."

Like Mockbee, Freear strongly defends and supports his students, but he also pushes them to extract their best efforts and drives himself to the point of exhaustion. Freear is "a bulldog," says David Buege. "Andrew is smart, brash, ambitious, always on the edge, often over-the-top, disciplined, deeply committed, self-confident. Someone without that confidence might well have failed. He's very respectful of Sambo and his legacy, but he's assertive about not being Sambo and the Rural Studio being more than Sambo."

Freear explains, "I'll never tell students 'no.' I'll put the issues in front of them. They'll listen and fight; it's wonderfully intense. And ninety-nine percent of the time they'll make the better decision. There's never one right decision. You give them a chance, and they'll want to do it to their best." He uses the growing collection of studio buildings as teaching tools—"an encyclopedia of projects," he calls them—and tries to draw lessons from nearly every act. "They learn that if they draw a two-by-four, some poor sucker is going to have to carry it from here to there. It's a heavy thing." Above all, Freear wants students to respect their clients and each other. "Working in teams is a great life experience. Apart from marriage you don't get it in life. I would like the students to think big, be ambitious for themselves and everyone else. I'd like them to love each other and walk away from here able to proceed and be bold, knowing that architects can make things happen."

Jay Sanders, Steve Hoffman's successor as second-year instructor from 2002 through the spring of 2004, describes Freear as "kind of an outlaw like Sambo was, in the sense that he pushes boundaries." The difference between him and Sambo, Sanders says, "is Andrew's taller and thinner and British."

You might think being British in rural Alabama would hamper getting along with the community. "Sambo had a southern way of dealing," says Winnie Cobb, proprietor of a bed and breakfast in Greensboro, the county seat. "He was educated but dropped very easily into the idiom of men in the South who live in small towns. He was very much at home with both races, spoke their language, and understood the meaning of things. He was so much a product of the very best that this part of the country has to offer. On the other hand, I don't know anyone who is like Sambo."

And then there is Freear, who, despite being foreign and speaking Yorkshire English (liberally sprinkled with y'alls), fits right in. "He understands that we're in a small southern town and you have to blend in, be something special but not upset the world we're living in," observes Ann Langford, the studio's longtime administrative assistant. "You're not going to be accepted if you ride a white horse into town to show poor backwards folks how it's done. Sambo didn't have that attitude, and neither does Andrew."

Moreover, in Hale County, Buege observes, "Everyone who doesn't have family going back to the time of the olive and wine colony is an outsider. It never occurred to Andrew that being foreign would be a disadvantage." Auburn Associate Professor David Hinson thinks that "Andrew being an outsider with a funny accent and a charming way gets a pass. He's seen as maybe not clued-in on some issues—not that he's insensitive." If you drive around Hale County with Freear, visiting Rural Studio projects in his big dual-axle truck, you will find him easy and natural with locals, and they with him, though his jokes sometimes baffle them. The ride with Freear will not be raucous, like a ride with Mockbee, filled with storytelling and fun; Freear lacks Mockbee's expansiveness, but he possesses a quieter charm and, like Mockbee, he is decent and kind and has a penchant for the outrageous.

The Program Expands

Since Mockbee's demise, a number of changes have occurred that have influenced especially the fifth-year students' community buildings, which are now the Rural Studio's central focus. During Mockbee's time, the university's financial support was intermittent and consisted mainly of his salary, requiring Mockbee to spend much of his time fundraising. Shortly after his death, Auburn committed $400,000 a year to the studio, endowing it with a measure of stability for the first time. Auburn's financial backing has permitted Freear to concentrate on students and projects and to build more durable structures.

There is a persistent threat, however, that Auburn will be forced to cut funding or, less probably, to eliminate it. Moreover, state laws prohibit university funds to be used for construction. Approximately $250,000 must be raised annually from private sources to cover building costs, according to Auburn's dean of architecture Daniel Bennett. To assure the studio's continuity it must build an endowment. Bruce Lindsey is in charge of fund-raising, but when prospective donors visit Hale County, they expect Freear—just as they once expected Mockbee—to show them around, answer their questions, and make a case for their donations. Outreach instructor John Forney (whom Freear calls his alter ego) and others are encouraging Freear to be more aggressive about raising funds. So far, he has not been able to pull away from the day-to-day pressures of teaching fifth year.

As the studio has matured, its community buildings have grown larger, more complex, more socially significant, and more numerous. During the early years, students built one house and, at most, two modest community buildings a year. During the two years following Mockbee's death, the studio completed seventeen projects dispersed over an area of 136 miles. Lindsey thinks that tackling so many assignments at once might have been "a bit of therapy for dealing with the loss of Sambo." Perhaps Freear, new and young, needed to prove something about the post-Mockbee studio, and about himself.

The pace and ambition of the projects grew punishing—and awesome. The year Mockbee died, the studio was working on a house plus five community projects. There was the Antioch Baptist Church, in the countryside about twenty-five miles northeast of Newbern; a senior center in Akron, twenty-five miles west of Newbern; a storefront in downtown Greensboro used by the Hale Empowerment and Reconstruction Organization (HERO) as a jobs center; and a park pavilion in Perry County, Hale's neighbor to the west and Alabama's poorest county. The pavilion for the newly opened Perry Lakes Park was the first phase of a three-year project, and the studio's first multiyear commitment. It was funded with $90,000 from the Alabama Department of Economic and

Mockbee's last design, called Lucy's House, was built with a tornado shelter as a family room, a tower, and walls of surplus carpet tiles.

Community Affairs. In addition, Mockbee's last design, called Lucy's House, was reinterpreted and built by outreach students. With surplus carpet tiles forming its exterior walls, Lucy's House is in Mason's Bend, the unpaved little settlement west of Newbern where the studio built its first two houses, the Haybale (1994) and the Butterfly (1997).

By increasing the number, size, and complexity of individual projects and the duration of its commitment to them, the studio more strongly established itself as a permanent institution in southwest Alabama. Fifth-year students once chose their own thesis projects, but now community leaders come to the studio seeking design and construction help. The Perry Lakes Park project was initiated by Probate Judge Donald Cook and Mayor Edward Daniel of Marion, Perry County's seat. When the directors of the Thomaston Rural Heritage Center received a grant to renovate their building and create a handful of jobs, they sought the studio's help. Similarly, Newbern's town fathers asked the studio to create a firehouse in their town.

The studio is more and more an economic boon for the region, says Greensboro bed-and-breakfast owner Cobb. "The outreach and fifth-year students rent apartments and buy groceries and materials," she observes. "People come and visit; they support restaurants. Looking back twenty years, who would have dreamed that in Newbern, Alabama, we'd have this dynamic group of young people adding something to the community? I think the studio is an inspiration for the local residents to do things for themselves."

The Level of Craft Improves

Freear notes that if the Rural Studio's approach to design and construction has changed, "It's because I said, 'We can make the craft better.'" He decries as "shanty architecture" the one-room "Pod" dwellings students built for themselves under the so-called "Supershed" on the studio's grounds. "I want to have high expectations for the students and the client. Why give them mediocre stuff when you can give them something really good? If we're going to make a glass box, the finish is going to be fantastic." Without question, it is the laboriously precise detailing that makes the Antioch Baptist Church (2002) a splendid little building. The same is true of the Perry Lakes Park Pavilion (2002) and the Thomaston Rural Heritage Center (2003).

Importantly, Freear has made the programming of buildings more precise. He wants to avoid the fate that has befallen the "windshield chapel" (2000) in Mason's Bend. The unfulfilled hope was that it would become a community center, housing a health facility and making computers and the Internet available to people in the area. Instead, the building has become an infrequently used chapel; no one owns it and no one takes care of it. In 2002, before his fifth-year students began designing the Akron Senior Center, Freear insisted that they determine the area's need for such a building, what its purpose should be, and who would manage it. He encourages communities to find their own funding for projects, believing that if they provide the money they are more likely to take ownership.

How It Works and How It Looks

Whereas wood and tin were once the studio's main material currency, steel now forms the sturdy structure of some of the large, new thesis projects. The use of hard-to-detail steel construction and Freear's insistence on very high standards of craft have refined the way projects are designed and have changed their appearance. Mockbee tended toward improvisation and letting buildings evolve on-site; Freear emphasizes getting things right before construction begins. Patrick Nelson, a fifth-year student in 2002–03, worked on the

Newbern Little League Baseball Field, a project of arched steel tubing spanned by catfish netting. "Andrew made us draw and draw and draw every corner, every detail," he says. "We also did computer modeling and collaging. He told us that the more we could solve in the studio, the less time we would have to waste on-site figuring out what comes next. We did a little less of that with Sambo; more was done on site." Freear insists that drawing saves time on-site and creates better communication among team members and between the team and the client. "I don't think that design/build should be a series of responses to screw-ups made earlier in the project," Freear says. "I believe in precision, not artfully camouflaged sloppiness."

But ratcheting up the level of craft, especially of complex structures, can pose problems. For one thing, it stretches out schedules. During the fall and early winter of 2002–03, Freear helped direct five projects by outreach students, converted the Red Barn in Newbern as the students' studio, and was responsible for four thesis projects: the Great Hall on the Newbern campus; the second phase of the Perry Lakes Park construction; the Newbern Little League Baseball Field; and the first phase of the Thomaston Rural Heritage Center, funded by a U.S. Department of Housing and Urban Development grant. "When they give you $190,000 of community money to build with, you suddenly get very grown up, uptight, and serious. You can't fail," observes Freear.

In his first year as the Rural Studio's co-director, Freear was faced with a diabolical mix of difficult projects, weather that delayed the start of construction, and slumping confidence as students became frustrated with the lengthy prebuilding process. At the end of the academic year, three of four thesis projects remained unfinished, and that summer and fall graduates had to return to finish their work—on their parents' penny. In September 2003, Freear found himself shepherding fifteen new thesis-project students in addition to twelve leftovers from the previous year.

By that time, Freear, Forney, and Lindsey began questioning the Rural Studio's operation. "I think 2002–03 established a benchmark of what you can't do," Forney says. They wondered if the studio should take on fewer projects, perhaps simpler ones. Should the studio's focus return to the rural house? But they realized that projects are unlikely to get simpler or smaller. For one thing, the students decide what and how to build, and each thesis group wants to create something bigger and more magnificent than last year's teams. Moreover, Freear, like Mockbee before him, is not one to lay down laws. Only three thesis projects were undertaken during 2003–04, but each was complex and problem-ridden.

The students themselves are already resolving some of the problems that plagued studio projects during the first two years after Mockbee's death. "This year—2004—there is a rejection of the steel and glass of last year," Freear says. "The students don't want to do something that's already been done, and they saw how much of the construction process was taken out of students' hands last year and the year before."

The thesis projects completed under Freear use some recycled materials, but you will find no hay bales, waste corrugated cardboard, windshields, or the like. Freear is more interested in creating buildings that are durable and will require minimal maintenance. A decline in the use of unconventional, scrappy materials would seem to go hand-in-hand with raising the bar.

As materials have changed, so has appearance. The Rural Studio's buildings under Mockbee were known for their striking angles, sharp diagonals, winged roofs, and idiosyncratic details. The new fifth-year projects tend toward a neutral, minimal modernism, a vocabulary that was not Mockbee's. With the exception of the stunning Perry Lakes Park Facilities, they are less iconoclastic and expressive. The new emphasis reflects Freear's roots in an English tradition of precision and contemporary craft. Forney observes, "It's been easy to work in that kind of language without feeling we're trying to conjure up the genie of Sambo. Where we get into trouble is that the language tends toward a kind of industrialism and aspires to levels of craftsmanship that students aren't always capable of."

Remember, however, these are not Freear's buildings. "I think there's a misperception about authorship of work," says Hinson, the Auburn professor. "People writing about the Rural Studio tend to think that it was Sambo's atelier, and that the students were executing Sambo's design. The students were always the authors. That's still the case. Sambo had the gift as

a teacher to empower his students to do high-quality work, and we're fortunate to have someone like Andrew who has a similar ability." Freear says he and his students engage in "few conversations about how things look. We talk about materials and the sustainability of materials, that our clients have no money or time to paint, that we shouldn't use a metal that's going to rust." He thinks each project looks different from the others. But they all bear his stamp: students everywhere imbibe (even if unconsciously) their teachers' predilections like mother's milk.

The buildings completed during the first three years under Freear's watch show a more sophisticated level of accomplishment than the studio's early work. The Perry Lakes Park Pavilion, with its gleaming roof floating in the trees, is transcendent. The glass office module in the Thomaston Rural Heritage Center is beautifully crafted. The Newbern Little League Baseball Field is brilliant in concept; its steel arches are low where children sit, rise to hold adults, and stretch out to create a dugout. But you may lament the absence of the winsome quirkiness that characterized Mockbee-era studio buildings.

You sense a little of that ebullient spirit and eccentric design in the works of the outreach program. It is there in student Cynthia Connolly's vegetable stand with movable walls of hog wire—a type of patchwork that uses chicken wire to stitch assorted metal leftovers. You intuit it in the pedicabs Richard Saxton put together to help the town of York clean its streets and in Lucy Begg's extension of an elderly woman's house. The smaller projects can more easily afford to be idiosyncratic.

The More Things Change…

Most of all, though, Mockbee's high-spirited and expressive-yet-relaxed approach lives on in the projects of the second-year program. Their vagaries since Mockbee's death underscore the observation that the studio is a moving target.

Steve Hoffman, who graduated from Auburn in 1997, returned to the studio one year later to teach second year. In his teaching methods, he took his cues from Mockbee, who, he says, "always talked about design, about letting students bite off as much as they could chew, about their learning teamwork and their own resourcefulness. He talked about kids

Students work on the Shiles House under a roof supported by poles. One wall is made of old tires filled with dirt and covered with cement.

coming home dirty and tired after learning to put in plumbing. That was a real Rural Studio kid."

When Hoffman started teaching, the studio was small and so were its projects. But the year Mockbee died, Hoffman's students were finishing the studio's largest and most ambitious residential project to date, a house for Shannon Sanders-Dudley. With a 1,500-square-foot ground floor, a 200-square-foot loft, and a complex program, it exceeded its budget and one-year schedule. In reaction, Hoffman set his sights lower in the fall of 2001, embarking on a 650-square-foot house for Tracy Shiles and her two teenage sons. Although the house was small and the family's requests minimal, the design got out of hand. Architecturally, the Shiles House is over-designed; it has too many materials, too many textures, too many shapes, angles, and emphases. "The first semester after Sambo's death, the void he left threw everything into confusion for me," Hoffman says. "I had problems admitting that the studio needed to change. I had a history there and loved it as it was. I felt if it had to change, I couldn't be there. I was torn."

Hoffman left the Rural Studio in 2002. He had spent nearly seven years there as a student and teacher, and he and Mockbee agreed that he needed to spread his wings. His successor was already in place. In September 2001, Mockbee had created a jack-of-all-trades position, clerk of works, to keep recent graduate Jay Sanders at the studio. As a fifth-year student, Sanders, a gregarious Texan, had worked on a new backstop for the Newbern baseball field. He had played on Newbern's team, had rented a warehouse in Greensboro and turned it into a community arts center, and had made many friends in the area. Sanders recalls that Mockbee firmed up his job offer the day before going into the hospital for the last time. "Sambo was wheezing and weak, and Steve, Andrew, and I took him to the student medical center in Auburn, and then to a cardiologist. When we got back here, he set me up to teach second year and also got Johnny [Parker] and Brenda Wilkerson [the studio's accountant] on permanent status. He tied up loose ends and went into the hospital the next morning."

Mockbee planned for Sanders to teach for only two years. "Sambo liked the idea of hiring second-year instructors who didn't know everything but were full of energy and believed they were capable of leadership," Sanders says. "Sambo figured he could put someone in this position for two-year periods and keep replacing them to keep the energy up." Sanders did not have teaching experience, but he sees his job as being less a teacher than a group leader or camp counselor. "I just guide the students in the right direction, make sure they work as a team, and keep the energy and momentum really high. They do all the design. People might worry about students making decisions, but if others make decisions for them, the students aren't as passionate about the work."

Like Hoffman, Sanders followed Mockbee's example, trying to make students aware of their own capacities, fueling their idealism, and teaching them basics. "They're terrible, absolutely terrible at the beginning, and they're so eager to build," Sanders told me in late 2003. "Yesterday, we were out on the site, none of them had a tool belt or tape measure, and they weren't getting anything done. Today, they're out there all working, all filthy, all have tool belts, and they're gaining confidence." The main thing he wants them to learn, he says, is that college is about becoming excited about

Justin Kelly, Jimmy Lee Matthews (Music Man), Jay Sanders, and Johnny Parker outside Sanders' Beacon Street studio

one's potential, not about getting a job. "Sambo knew that going through this experience at this age made students kinda' snake bit. He knew he was going to hear from these guys again."

Like Mockbee and Freear, Sanders has an easy way with people, and his students emulate him. "My students walk into the neighborhood and talk to everybody on their front porches, and they know everybody's name," Sanders says. His main project accomplishment is the 2003 house for Jimmy Lee Matthews, known to all as Music Man. "The Lord sent Mr. Jay to me," Music Man says, and Sanders calls Music Man "a pure heart person." Sanders told me that he and the thirty-two students who have worked on Music Man's house "don't care if the house gets pushed off the hill. We've had more fun with Music Man than anything." Music Man has decorated his walls and refrigerator with photos of the students, and he created a little monument to them on his property. It is composed of wood crosses and boards, each representing a student, each bearing a phrase or two. One reads, "Mr. Garth, if he can help peoples he will do it. He got love in his heart. I thank Jesus, Holy Ghost for him."

Music Man's House returned the studio to its roots. As with the studio's first house for Shepard and Alberta Bryant, middle-class white students and an impoverished black

One of three unusual toilets the studio created in Perry Lakes Park

client worked closely together, became good friends, and crossed a threshold to a previously feared and unfamiliar world. "The success of those relationships, like with Alberta and Shepard, was as important to Sambo as anything," Sanders recalls.

Music Man came to the studio's attention after his trailer caught fire and the studio's administrative assistant, Ann Langford, heard that he had moved into a donated, wrecked trailer without running water. During the studio's early days, students chose clients from a list drawn up by the Hale County Department of Human Resources. Nowadays, clients seek out the studio or are chosen by faculty or staff who have come to understand that client selection is not an appropriate job for students.

For his final project before leaving in the spring of 2004, Sanders and his students designed and built a modular, 1,000-square-foot house that Sanders hopes may replace the region's omnipresent trailer. The house for the Patrick family consists of a steel frame, the bays of which can be filled with any material at hand. The Patrick House uses standard wood-frame construction. How does it escape looking as ordinary as a trailer? The students tailored it for the client and site, twisting it to spare existing trees, and capping it with a wacky hat. "My goal is that others in the community, seeing that it was easy to put together, would build their own version of the Patrick House," Sanders says.

The Maturing Studio

You might conclude that the Rural Studio has evolved into a less unified entity than it was in its early days. Complex community buildings have replaced the simple rural house as the studio's mainstay, and second-year and fifth-year programs have followed dissimilar design paths. Freear has tried to counter this trend by bringing all students together in a new studio, the converted Red Barn, and for communal dinners and lectures.

In earlier years, fifth-year students found their own small thesis projects and often their own materials and funding; now, town and county leaders approach the studio with large projects they want designed and built, usually with government funds. As the size and complexity of such projects has increased, the level of programming and detailing has become more sophisticated. Many mature architects would gladly accept commissions like the Perry County Lakes Park Pavilion or the Thomaston Rural Heritage Center. Architect Jim Adamson, a partner in the firm Jersey Devil and frequently an invited critic for studio projects, says, "It's an amazing experience for these students, and they are producing very high level work and getting a very solid foundation."

The second-year program has changed little; it cannot change much, since second-year students have more enthusiasm than ability and stay at the studio for only a semester. By fifth year, students have learned a lot, and they have a year to work on a building. "It's calmer, more grown up," Freear says. But fifth year also has grown more frenetic as projects have become larger and more complex. And there is the rub: how do you balance the studio's evolution toward more ambitious, big-time buildings against a wish to retain its rural soul? How can the studio maintain Sambo Mockbee's childlike sense of fun and adventure while laboring on very adult, multiyear, high-pressure projects? How can it remain intimate in size and spirit yet capable of successfully tackling big projects? The answer is, Freear says, "You can't choreograph it. These opportunities come up and you have to take them. Beggars can't be choosers."

In the meanwhile, Freear, John Forney, Bruce Lindsey, Jay Sanders, the students, and outside critics talk a lot about the studio's future, whether it should cut back, perhaps, or return to basics. Forney says he has tried to steer his outreach students back to simpler buildings to avoid "the death-march struggles that the thesis projects have sometimes turned into. Nevertheless, I very much admire Andrew's desire to get the thesis projects to be more socially significant and challenging. I think that's pushed the Rural Studio to places it hasn't been before. I don't know what our model should be."

Sanders observes that "Sambo never had a master plan for this place. Maybe his legacy is that it will live on without him, without me, without Andrew, without the students that knew him. If it continues to move forward, in ten years it may not feel anything like it does today." For the present, Freear and his gang will continue to "proceed and be bold," in Mockbee's words. And Sambo would love it.

Thomaston Rural Heritage Center: a new glass box in a refurbished old building

RURAL STUDIO
REACTS TO ITS LOSS

THE ACADEMIC YEAR 2001–02 was highly emotional. On December 30, 2001, a soul-chilling day in Jackson, Mississippi, Samuel Mockbee, the Rural Studio's founding heart and guiding spirit, died of leukemia. Three days later, students and faculty gathered for his funeral ninety miles east of Jackson in Meridian, the city of his birth and childhood. That January, they came together at Auburn University to honor his talent and humanity. In March, New York's Max Protetch Gallery held a memorial, and in May, Hale County said its goodbye at the annual pig roast, when the studio sends off its new graduates. Mockbee's childhood friend B. B. (G. William) Archer presented the keynote, and three Hale County crop dusters flew over the event in missing-man formation. During the third flight, one plane peeled away toward Mississippi.

D. K. Ruth, the studio's co-founder, oversaw a group of outreach students who interpreted and built Mockbee's last design, called Lucy's House. Steve Hoffman spent his last year as second-year instructor supervising his students' work on Tracy Shiles's new home. And fifth-year students, under Andrew Freear, finished a wide range of projects, including the Antioch Baptist Church. The studio was determined to "proceed and be bold," as Mockbee had frequently admonished.

It was also a breakthrough year for museum exhibitions. In the fall, the studio displayed work at Cincinnati's Contemporary Arts Center, for which faculty and students built a dome of hay bales, a templelike structure out of carpet tiles, and a theater from waste corrugated cardboard. In March, the Whitney Biennial in New York City included work by the studio. "That was huge for us," Freear says, because the studio was one of only three architects ever invited to the event. To top off the year's accomplishments, in the summer of 2002, the studio had an exhibition at NeoCon, the annual design trade fair in Chicago.

LUCY'S HOUSE

2002

IN THE SPRING of 2001, when Sambo Mockbee showed me a preliminary drawing for Lucy's House, it had three major elements: a single-story living area, a screened porch, and a simple tower containing the master bedroom upstairs and, a few steps below grade, a tornado shelter that would double as a family room. He had always left the design of Rural Studio buildings to students, but this scheme was different: it would be part of a 2001 exhibit of the Rural Studio's work in Chicago, sponsored by a carpet manufacturer that was considering donating materials to the studio. Mockbee was excited about what he called the design's "big hit"—exterior walls made of stacked and compressed surplus carpet tiles. Describing the family room/ tornado shelter, he said, "Spatially, it'll be cavelike, a mystical space." The shelter turned out as Mockbee described it. But the porch is missing from Lucy's House, and the originally simple tower turned into a twisting alignment of burgundy-colored triangles sheathed in plywood and coated with waterproofing.

Such changes are not unusual for the studio. Designs invariably undergo alterations during construction, and Mockbee encouraged his students to find their own solutions. The overwrought, crumpled tower most likely reflects students' desires to make "more architecture," Freear says. The work, supervised by Auburn architecture professor D. K. Ruth (now retired), was carried out by seven outreach students, six of whom were architecture students.

Lucy's House is in Mason's Bend, a backwater of shanties and trailers along a dirt road about twenty-five miles northwest of Newbern. It is home to one of the Rural Studio's most striking buildings, a 2000 community center-cum-chapel, whose hefty, low rammed-earth walls are topped with a glass roof made of surplus Chevy Caprice windshields. Mason's Bend is where the studio built its first house in 1994, the Haybale House for Shepard and Alberta Bryant, and its second, the 1997 Butterfly House for Anderson and Ora Lee Harris. When Mockbee decided to build a new house for the Bryants' daughter Lucy and her husband, who is the Harrises' son, they were living in the shanty that the elder Harrises vacated when they moved into the Butterfly House. It was "mighty crampy" for her family of five, Lucy says.

The super-insulated walls of Lucy's House are made of 72,000 individually stacked carpet tiles, each about fifteen-by-fifteen inches. The students stabilized the tiles with thin steel columns, capped the stacks with a heavy wooden ring beam, and applied pressure to post-tension the tiles into a dense mass that repels water and fire. The carpet had been warehoused long enough to completely off-gas noxious fumes, Freear says, and had been treated to prevent microbiological growth.

Like its predecessors, Lucy's House, built for $32,000, was a gift to its owners. Its architecture is conceptually modern, albeit nudged and tweaked by southern rural forms—sheds, barns, trailers—and the exigencies of southwest Alabama's perennial heavy rains and scorching summer sun. To help keep the non-air-conditioned living area temperate, the house faces east, as does its only large window—a bay shaded by an overhanging slanted roof. There are only a few small openings on the rear elevation, where three children's bedrooms are lined up. Ceiling fans circulate air through the living area and over a low wall into the children's rooms, while an attic fan vents hot air.

What Lucy Harris likes best about her new house, she says, is lying in bed at night looking up at the North Star, which is framed by a skylight built to Mockbee's specifications. Does Lucy like her "whacked-out tower," as Freear calls it? "It's unique. I love it," she says. And she does not miss a porch, never having had one. But if Mockbee had been around, he would have given her a screened porch, and "He probably would have made the tower simpler," says Freear.

Unlike the Rural Studio–built Hay Bale and Butterfly houses,
also located in Mason's Bend, Lucy's House stands isolated from
the little settlement, its only neighbor the adjacent trailer owned
by a relative.

Lucy Harris and her family lived in this house (which she called
"mighty crampy") when Mockbee suggested she needed a new one.

The walls are made of leftover carpet tile; 72,000 tiles, each
fifteen inches square, were individually stacked, stabilized with
steel poles, capped with a heavy wood ring beam, and post-
tensioned into a dense mass.

To keep the house cool, its only large opening faces east and is shaded by an overhanging shed roof. The tower, simple in Samuel Mockbee's early sketches, became twisted and overly dramatic when built

The translucent wall framing the front door admits daylight and
gives shadowed glimpses of life within.

Lucy Harris relaxes in her living room.

The tower bedroom overlooks the living area.

The skylight in the tower bedroom frames the North Star.

One of the three children's rooms

Mockbee envisioned the below-grade tornado shelter and family
room as "a cavelike space," which it is.

SHILES HOUSE

2002

MOST TOURS OF Rural Studio buildings bypass the Shiles House, located about nine miles west of Newbern. It suffers from overeagerness by its student-architects, who lavished on it an overabundance of ideas, forms, materials, and finishes. The problem with all second-year projects, Freear says, "is that the students are like sixteen independent orchestra conductors, and they all want to do something different."

Students chose Tracy Shiles and her two boys as clients in 2001, the last time a second-year group selected a client. Shortly thereafter, the studio's professors decided client selection was not an appropriate responsibility for twenty-year-olds; it has since become a faculty and staff responsibility. Shiles was living "in abhorrent conditions—bad landlord, holes in the floor, snakes came in, no heat," says Steve Hoffman, the second-year instructor at the time. Her demands were modest. She asked the studio to "put as much distance between my boys and me as possible," and she wanted two features she had seen in earlier Rural Studio houses, an open kitchen that steps up from the living room and a window seat in her bedroom.

The students' first move was to create a frame of telephone poles and top them with a roof that sheltered the students when working in bad weather. The house is in a flood plain, so it is raised on footings, and one wall is made of old tires filled with dirt and covered in chicken wire and cement. The students took their cue from the much-photographed Yancey Chapel (1995), also called the tire chapel, in Sawyerville. Much of the Shiles House is clad in oak shingles cut from used shipping pallets. For the roof, the students cut up leftover insulated door panels.

The house type is a modified dogtrot, with kitchen and sunken living area on one side of the ground floor and Shiles's bedroom on the other. The boys' rooms are on the second-floor mezzanine, to which a stair climbs on the tire wall. A window wall, with panes in assorted shapes and sizes, edges the curving stair and continues to the entry, creating a transparent corner. Hoffman considers the corner and the "funky use of tires" the building's "big hits."

The exterior, with its abundance of shapes, roof angles, and cladding materials, is the result, says Andrew Freear, of sixteen students all wanting to do something different.

Tracy Shiles now shares her home with another family.

A stair, flanked by windows, curves around the sunken living
area, ascending the tire wall.

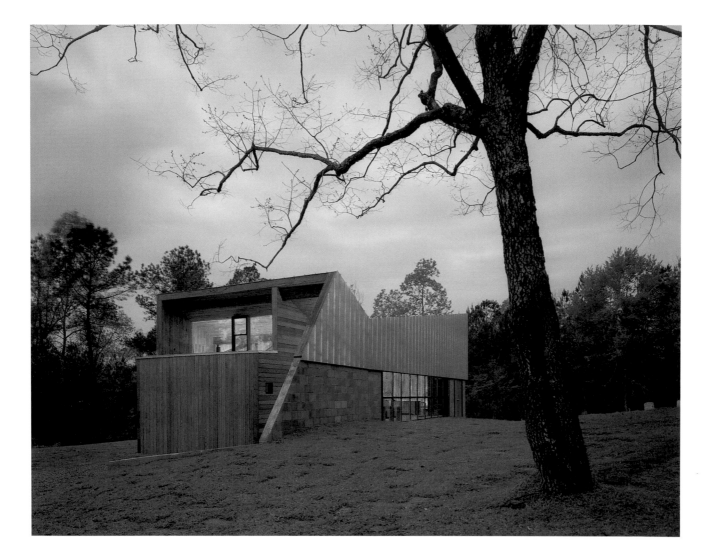

ANTIOCH BAPTIST CHURCH

2002

THE ANTIOCH BAPTIST CHURCH is a reincarnation of sorts. It replaces a disintegrating century-old country church with an equally minimalist but modern structure. The students wanted their building to be as simple as its predecessor and reused about eighty percent of the old church's materials. Rainwater was eroding the existing church's footings and, because it was so dilapidated and had neither a bathroom nor a baptismal font, its small congregation was drifting away. Freear believes that the new church, located about twenty-five miles north-northeast of Newbern, helped the community sustain part of its culture. He says a young church member, Cedric Caddell, asked him to build "the Cadillac of churches." In part, Freear wanted his students, most of them pretty religious, to experience black church culture.

Freear believed that if church members had to worship elsewhere during construction, they might never return. So he and his team built a temporary chapel, using metal from the existing roof. Around the chapel they stacked materials they had salvaged when dismantling the old church, cataloging and counting every nail and screw. They recycled roof and floor joists, wood paneling, tongue-and-groove boards, and exterior corrugated metal.

To protect the new galvanized-aluminum–clad building from the heavy rain wash that had undermined the old church, the students sited it higher on the hillside than its predecessor and designed its entrance wall, supported by hand-built metal and wood trusses, to double as a retaining wall that diverts rainwater from the building. They put a scupper on the roof to channel water onto a concrete receiver on the ground, and they surrounded the church with gravel, rather than soil that could wash away.

The students filled the twenty-by-forty-five-foot building's metal structure with wood in two interlocking, wrapping forms. One wrap runs north-south and covers the solid south wall and the ceiling and extends to the glazed north wall. The second wrap shapes the baptistery on the west, the pastor's room, and a restroom on the east. The interior's main design feature consists of a large north-facing window wall that gives congregants an eye-level view of their old graveyard. To keep the little church cool in the summer, the students left the south wall windowless, and they cut three small, rectangular openings at the floor's edges to admit cool air from the crawl space. Ceiling fans circulate air, and operable clerestories allow hot air to escape. The church cost $35,000, $10,000 of which was raised by the congregation. A donation by a Birmingham developer provided glass for the building, and old concrete blocks from renovated women's dorms at Auburn were employed as footings. "I love the idea that blocks that were holding up beds for middle-class students are holding up a little black church in the middle of Perry County," Freear says.

In replacing a simple country church, the students wanted to create an equally plain building, and they reused materials from the old church.

To protect the galvanized–aluminum–clad building from stormwater that eroded the old church's footings, students positioned it higher on the hillside and erected an entrance retaining wall.

Enclosing the mostly metal structure are two applications of
wood—one extending from the solid south wall to the north-
facing window wall, the other reaching over the baptistery to the
rear of the church.

The glazed north wall overlooks an old community cemetery.

UNDER ANDREW FREEAR, THE PACE INTENSIFIES

THE YEAR 2001–02 saw an escalation of the studio's workload, Freear's fifth-year projects accounting for most of the increase. With the blessings of the studio's faculty and staff, he had unofficially assumed leadership and wanted to prove the studio could survive its founder's death. Doubtlessly, he also wanted to prove himself, and hard work helped dull the pain of Mockbee's loss for everyone. Each of the new projects marked a turning point of sorts.

The HERO (Hale Empowerment Rehabilitation Organization) Storefront was the studio's first contribution to downtown Greensboro, a county seat whose downtown is fifty percent vacant. In downtown Akron, fifth-year students refurbished a Depression-era building as a senior center. The megaphone-shaped Perry Lakes Park Pavilion, with its gleaming metal roof that appears to float in the woods, was the first phase of the studio's multi-year project and the first in a series of buildings framed in steel. For better and worse, they required meticulous drawings and fabrication by professionals. More work from the outreach studio, including a one-room addition for an elderly couple, continued the studio's tradition of completely hands-on architecture.

The new crop of buildings was impressive, especially because the Rural Studio could easily have faltered or failed after Mockbee's death. Freear had kept the studio's body and soul together, and, at the end of 2002, Auburn awarded him tenure and appointed him co-director of the studio with Bruce Lindsey, head of architecture.

HERO STOREFRONT

2002

SINCE WALKER EVANS and James Agee visited Greensboro, Hale County's seat, during the Depression and described it in *Let Us Now Praise Famous Men*, little has changed. In the 1930s Agee wrote, "The little towns, the county seats, house by house white-painted . . . stand so prim, so voided, so undefended upon starlight." Greensboro's Main Street still looks abandoned; about half its storefronts stand empty, and the few shoppers you see tend to be elderly. So a newly rehabbed storefront with a softly modern canopy of stainless chain metal—found by students while dumpster diving in Montgomery—is a hopeful sign.

The HERO Storefront marked the first time that the Rural Studio has been let loose on Main Street, Greensboro, a traditionally conservative town. When the students began renovating the twenty-five-by-seventy-five-foot, double-height structure, they realized that the brick facade was so fragile it needed bracing. Their solution was to sandwich it between double sets of steel columns. They recessed a new glass wall beneath the masonry and made the rear wall of glass, too. As a result, you can stand on Main Street and see through the building to HERO's small campus and the Children's Center the studio built there in 1999. For now, the nonprofit is using the storefront as an employment center. In the future, it hopes to convert the fully wired structure into a "knowledge café" that makes computers and the Internet available to the region's residents.

The students left the building's exterior as they found it and added only minor touches inside: a storage wall that screens restrooms, a kitchenette, and a couple of very high-backed chairs in the waiting area. The back of each chair contains a computer workstation. The students blackened the ceiling with expansion board— which is usually employed between panels of concrete on sidewalks—and hung bare bulbs from rigid, wriggly wires. The studio's main job was to clean the building and dismantle its accretions, thereby "revealing its real character," says Freear. The students removed ceilings to expose roof joists and cleaned the walls to reveal a sweep of green-painted stucco. This swath of color moves your eye from the front through the rear glazing to a little garden whose ruinlike walls form a courtyard paved with donated stone. Also donated was the tempered glass used for walls and doors.

The most appealing features of the storefront are its transparency and its no-frills blending of existing brick walls with new, sleek glass and metal walls. The rehabilitation cost about $25,000.

With its friendly yet modern chain metal canopy, the HERO
Storefront is a welcome newcomer in downtown Greensboro,
where half the buildings stand vacant.

Interior work consisted mainly of cleaning the building and removing its partition walls and dropped ceilings to expose roof joists. Workstations fit into the back of student-designed high-backed chairs.

At back, a ruinlike wall creates a little courtyard. Just beyond is
the studio-built HERO Children's Center of 1999.

AKRON SENIOR CENTER

2002

AS A TOWN, Akron is the back of beyond. Located at the dead end of an obsolete rail line on the Black Warrior River, about twenty-six miles northwest of Newbern, Akron briefly thrived during the late nineteenth century when transportation was dominated by railroads and waterways. But once trucking and automobiles took over, Akron, which is inaccessible by highway, languished. In 1996 the Rural Studio erected a riverside pavilion that is used for reunions, picnics, and other outdoor Akron events. In 2000 the studio built the Boys and Girls Club in Akron's ramshackle downtown, and in the fall of 2001 four fifth-year students— Jonathan Graves, Matthew Barrett, Breanna Hinderliter, and Joseph Yeager—began work on a place for seniors to congregate. Their first step was to gauge, with help from local churches, the need for such a facility. Graves says they found at least ninety-eight elderly people living within a twenty-five-mile radius of Akron

The town offered the students several unbuilt sites, but they chose a Depression-era former retail building and decided to turn its right half into a senior center, the other half into a community center. The 2,800-square-foot building was the largest the studio had worked with. Freear says that "its very good watertight roof" convinced him the project was doable. After tearing off a wooden shop front and cutting two entrances into the facade, the students' work entailed mostly interior design.

They left the community center as an undivided space topped by a metal ceiling, painted the ceiling and walls, and sanded the hardwood floors. Graves persuaded the president of a Wisconsin company that makes bifold aircraft hangar doors to reengineer an eleven-by-twelve-foot version for use as the community center's front door, and to donate it. When open, the big door forms an entrance canopy.

Over in the senior center, the students took down a metal ceiling, exposed and sandblasted the heavy wooden trusses, and put in a new wood floor. A subtle feature, Graves points out, is the way they cut the skylight to flood the walls with diffused light during lunch at noon.

The governing idea for the senior center was to give the community and its elders abundant contact with each other. The center's heart is an elegant, 350-square-foot, new glass-enclosed porch. There, people play bingo or dominos and chat while keeping an eye on activity in the street. The scale and rhythm of the porch's bays were determined by the dimension of donated glass, which was tempered and therefore could not be cut without cracking or shattering.

The Akron Senior Center, run by an organization called Golden Years, is now probably the busiest place in town. Each morning, as many as thirty-five older citizens arrive. They play games or chew the fat for an hour, then they are served lunch. Shortly thereafter, everyone goes home, body and soul replenished.

The long-vacant downtown building, before the studio began
renovations

The center's heart is a glazed porch with views of the street.
Here seniors say grace before lunch.

Skylights were cut to brighten the walls with sunlight at lunchtime.

PERRY LAKES PARK PAVILION

2002

THE PAVILION MARKS the first step in the Rural Studio's reclamation of a 600-acre park, the only public outdoor recreation area in Alabama's poorest county, Perry. Located about twenty-five miles northeast of Newbern, Perry Lakes Park was created by the Depression-era Works Progress Administration. A drowning in the lake, along with the general neglect that may have allowed it, led to its closing in the 1970s; the dedication of a probate judge jump-started its reopening in 2002. For twelve years Judge Donald Cook sought grants to refurbish the park, and in 2001 he obtained $90,000 from the Alabama Department of Economic and Community Affairs. Cook, a white judge, formed a board of directors that included Edward Daniel, the black mayor of Marion, the county seat. "It was great to watch small-town politics and see how black and white people *are* getting along," says Jennifer Bonner, one of three team members who designed and built the pavilion.

Bonner explains that the pavilion is meant to be "an icon that says the park is back." It is used for catfish fries and family reunions, and serves as an outdoor classroom for nearby Judson College. Visually, the megaphone-shaped pavilion is serenity itself. Its shimmering, undulating aluminum roof, rising to twenty-four feet and dipping to seven, appears to float in the trees above a cedar floor. Black steel columns, with concrete footings that are imprinted with bark and wood chips, are different heights and blend with the trunks of moss-draped live oaks, cypresses, and tupelos. Four fingerlike prongs top the columns and support the roof beam.

For the pavilion's flooring and furniture the students wanted to use cedar, which does not need to be treated, weathers well, and is durable. When Mary Ward Brown, an elderly local author, donated a cedar thicket from her property, "We all took chain saws and Andrew's truck and the second-year students cut down trees and took them to be milled in Greensboro," Bonner says. Because the ground surrounding the pavilion is swampy, the architect-builders lifted its deck a foot and a half off the ground and spread a layer of wood chips beneath it to repel mosquitoes. The deck wraps back to a seven-foot-high wall that shields a ramp for people with disabilities and visually anchors the composition. The pavilion cost $25,000.

Revealing, perhaps, as much about his artistic predilections as about the pavilion, Freear says, "I like this because it's cool and calm. So many of the past Rural Studio details just hit you in the face." Bonner remarks, "The idea was all about the landscape." Her team placed the benches, she says, "so that you're looking out onto a paw paw patch and the landscape beyond."

The pavilion marked the first phase of a three-stage project that
reclaimed a park closed since 1970.

The undulating aluminum roof is supported by black columns
that blend with nearby tree trunks. A local author let students
cut from her property some cedar trees to use for flooring.

The "kissing bench" is behind a seven-foot wall, which shields a
ramp for disabled visitors. From here, the pavilion opens toward
the front, megaphone style.

The pavilion is used for catfish fries and family reunions, and
serves as an outdoor classroom.

ROOM FOR ESSIE AND JAB

2002

THE RURAL STUDIO calls the room that Jody Touchstone built for Essie and Jab Williams an architectural ambulance. "I was working on a program to allow sick, older people to stay in their homes," says Touchstone, a fifth-year student in 2001–02. She began with small jobs—putting in a hand rail or a wheelchair ramp, redesigning a door. Then a home health nurse presented her with the problem of an elderly patient suffering from a brain tumor and living in terrible conditions. "On my first visit we walked around their house," Touchstone recalls. "Almost all the windows were broken—they put plastic over them in the winter. The roof leaked, you could see through the floor to the ground in places, and there was no insulation in any part of the house." She considered simply insulating the Williams's room, but "the foundations had been sinking for a while, and rotting beams were everywhere."

Touchstone wanted to build a simple structure that could be easily replicated by unskilled laborers and could be built quickly. "Because these are sick, old people, if you want to make their life better you need to do it right away," she says. In eleven weeks, she built Essie and Jab "a room and bathroom that are dry and warm and that they could get in and out of easily," she says.

Wishing to change the original house as little as possible, she tore down only two derelict appendages, a lean-to containing a washer and dryer, which she moved inside, and an archaic bathroom with bad plumbing. In their place she put a new, insulated room warmed by a propane heater and a bathroom that includes a wheelchair-accessible shower. She built a new foundation for her addition, which is separated from the main house by a roofed corridor. Touchstone built the room and bath, using some donated materials, for $4,500.

Essie and Jab, an ailing, elderly couple, in their former
main room

The white shelves were built by Touchstone.

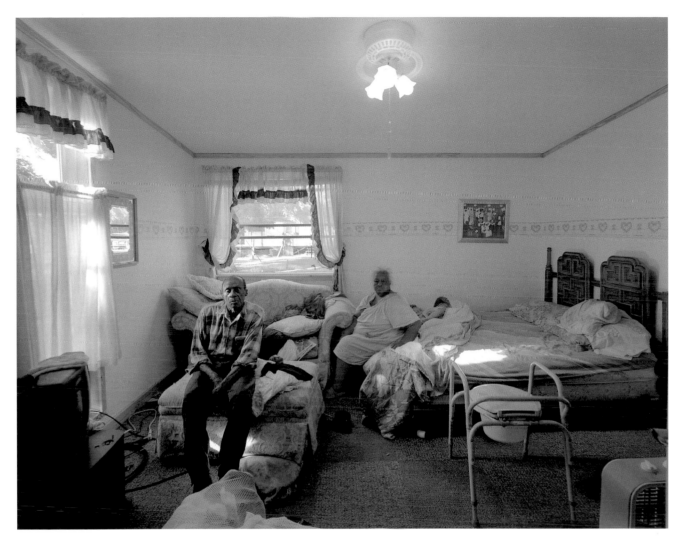

Essie and Jab in their new room

PERSONALIZED PROJECTS BOTH BIG AND SMALL

FREEAR'S FIRST IMPULSE upon becoming co-director was to bring together second-year, fifth-year, and outreach students, who lived apart and worked in scattered studios. In late summer, Freear, along with construction supervisor Johnny Parker, newly installed second-year instructor Jay Sanders, and a handful of inmates on work release from the nearby Farquhar Cattle Ranch, picked up hammers and nails and converted the Red Barn—a boarded-up, rusted-tin storehouse—into a studio for everyone.

Other projects followed, each different from the last, each adding a new dimension to the studio's work. The second-year students' house for Music Man (a.k.a. Jimmy Lee Matthews) was as dynamic and idiosyncratic as the client, who paid tribute to Sanders and his students by creating an outdoor "museum" of wooden crosses bearing inscriptions about his architects.

The studio finished three toilets for Perry Lakes Park, perhaps the most visually striking outdoor restrooms in the U.S. Each has a different shape and a different view, but all are of stainless steel and cedar. Equally quirky is the Newbern Little League Baseball Field, with its backstop of metal arches that range from child-size to seventeen feet in height and are spanned with catfish netting. The fifth-year students' final undertaking in 2003–04 was the Thomaston Rural Heritage Center, a renovation for a huge, ugly 1950s building, into which the studio inserted a pristine glass and metal box for offices and display space.

In December 2002, Auburn posthumously awarded Mockbee, along with former Secretary of State Madeleine Albright, its Lifetime Achievement Award. The awards presentation was held at the United Nations Headquarters in New York. At one point during their visit, students, faculty, and family crowded into a limousine, and Mockbee's youngest child, Julius, leaned out and shouted, "war eagle," Auburn's victory cry.

March saw an exhibit of Rural Studio work in Vienna, and Freear used the occasion to lecture there and in London and Berlin. In June, it was Barcelona. Freear, clerk of works Jennifer Bonner, fifth-year students Jermaine Washington and Patrick Nelson, and a half dozen students from the Barcelona School of Architecture built exhibition rooms made of hay bales and carpet tiles and two unusual walls: one of polyester clothing scraps, the other of brick-sized, compressed tin cans.

The 2002–03 thesis projects were larger and more complex than ever, and because Freear insisted on improved craft and precise drawings, fifth-year students missed their schedules. The delays and the use of steel construction, requiring professional fabricators, provoked painful self-examination and criticism. Both were cut short by a reliable self-correcting mechanism: students. The following year, they vetoed the use of steel, and with the faculty decided to build fewer projects and work closer to home.

RED BARN

2003

WHEN I FIRST saw the Red Barn it was a rusted, pockmarked, weatherworn thing, its windows sealed with strips of tin and rusted metal. The building is a favorite subject for photographer William Christenberry, an Alabama native transplanted to Washington, D.C., who has visited Hale County each summer for the last three decades to document the aging process of buildings from his youth. Jay Sanders says that when he was a second-year student, "There were rumors that the building had been a brothel, a movie theater, and a lot of other things. Apparently it was a hay barn." Along with the post office and G.B. Mercantile, the two-story Red Barn *is* downtown Newbern.

In the summer of 2002, Freear, Sanders, the studio's construction supervisor Johnny Parker, and inmates on work release from the Farquhar Cattle Ranch started prying the former hay barn open and rehabbing it as a design studio. At the time, the second-year students were making do drawing on the kitchen table at Morrisette House (the farmhouse that served as the studio's hub), while fifth-year students employed a small building nearby as a studio. Freear, who was concerned by the "lack of communication between the older and younger students," wanted a single place where everyone could work. Jennifer Bonner remembers that all the students pitched in. "It was an orientation project of sorts." They cleaned the building out and put in a stair, which they fireproofed and enclosed with drywall. They hung windows and new shutters, wired the building, and installed fans and fluorescents. Downstairs they built a bathroom, an air-conditioned computer room, a darkroom, and a tiny laundry.

Today, the Red Barn's exterior is still a rusty patchwork, but its windows are glazed and usually open, and the building has become the Rural Studio's academic hub. "The Red Barn is lit up every night," Freear says. "It's pretty much the center of Newbern now."

William Christenberry, *Facade of Warehouse, Newbern, Alabama,* 1981

Two of William Christenberry's photographs show the state of the
barn some twenty years before the studio took it on.

The Rural Studio pried open the Red Barn, admitting light and life.

Andrew Freear (second from right) comments on students' work

A pig roast on parade outside of the Red Barn

MUSIC MAN'S HOUSE

2003

TWELVE MILES NORTHWEST of Greensboro off County Road 19, you come to a driveway lined with handmade signs, "Don't come at night. Too much goin' on. Trust nobody but God, Jesus, Holy Ghost." As you read "Dogs Bad," intimating a dangerous alarm system, four friendly, tail-wagging canines approach. The eighteen-acre property beyond belongs to Jimmy Lee Matthews, known to all as Music Man. He inherited the land from his mother, who inherited it from her employer, whose nanny she was. Past the property's hog wire gate—a patchwork of plastic and tin odds and ends found on the site—are four tumbledown structures. One house belonged to Music Man's late mother, another to his uncle, and there are two burnt-out trailers. Music Man had been living in one of the trailers, given to him after a tree fell on his own.

"Music Man totally shatters our preconceptions about poverty," says Jay Sanders, the instructor who oversaw the design of a new home for him. "You wouldn't expect someone who lived in such conditions to be so excited about every day." Sanders believes that getting to know this very poor but optimistic and enterprising African-American was more instructive for his class of middle-class, white southern students than the building process. "We loved him to death," Sanders says.

Among the students' first moves was to bring in a septic system and fill in a dry well. On top of the covered well Music Man created his museum. It consists of wooden crosses and boards bearing handmade inscriptions, one for almost every student who worked on his house. Music Man says their arrival was "a miracle from God." The first cross he installed reads, "Jay Sanders and Mr. Sambo is two good mens God put on earth, Amen." Sanders and Music Man became each others' biggest fans, and Sanders says he and his students wanted to build a house "as dynamic as Music Man." That and an attempt to control Music Man's mania for collecting things shaped the design. "Because Music Man is an accumulator of junk, the students made the room so high he couldn't fill it up," says Sanders.

The tall, narrow, 600-square-foot house is a typical dogtrot, its entry porch screened with hog wire and one of its walls filled with old colored bottles. The interior is divided into two major spaces, one for living and sleeping; the other, for bathroom activities, overlooks a ravine. The living area is an undivided space, very high and very glassy at each end. The students wanted to emulate a storage system they had seen in a Quaker house, where chairs and other objects were hung on wall pegs when not in use. The pegs, Sanders says, changed to "everything rolls"—that is, to a system in which furniture, including the bed, can glide along a lateral brace. It allows

Music Man to move his bed closer to the stove in winter and under the fan in summer. "We talked about a room for his spirit. It becomes a room for air," which is moved by a powerful fan in the front wall. Sanders' thinking was that keeping furniture in motion and raised off the floor would discourage Music Man from cluttering his home.

When I last visited, unannounced, the space was tidy and clean. Music Man had divided the open space into four areas, separated by five television sets. The walls and refrigerator door were adorned with pictures of the students, and there were bright red curtains over the rear window. Sanders explains that when he asked Music Man what kind of curtains he would like, "He said he wanted curtains that parted like the Red Sea."

On the back of the living area is a curved space containing the bathroom. From both the shower stall and the toilet the students provided broad views of the property, because Music Man takes both bathing and elimination very seriously, Sanders explains. The wet room, as Sanders calls it, was intended as the little dwelling's main attraction.

The students found many of the materials—timber, chicken wire, old bottles— on the property itself. Other materials, such as glass and the cedar that lines the interior, were donated. The total cost—including the septic system, tool shed, and landscaping—was $28,000. "It probably cost too much for a house this size," Sanders says. He blames not materials but mistakes. Call them opportunities for learning.

Amid tumbledown structures, Music Man created his museum of
wooden crosses and boards. On them he wrote inscriptions about
his architects.

A gap in the property's hog wire gate, made by folk artist Butch
Anthony and Rural Studio students, allows Music Man to ride
through on his motorcycle.

During construction, Music Man lived in a Rural Studio–built tool shed on his property. The mural on the right is by Samantha Rinehart Taylor.

The tall, 600-square-foot dwelling's front porch is enclosed with
hog wire, plastic, and tin found on the site.

Furniture glides along a lateral brace, allowing Music Man to change the configuration of his space; it also prevents him from cluttering it.

The house's "big hit" is the curved, corrugated metal-clad
bathroom at the rear.

At the back, the so-called "wet room" has translucent dividers.

Music Man uses television sets to partition his space into four areas.

PERRY LAKES PARK FACILITIES

2003

FROM THE RURAL STUDIO—DESIGNED pavilion, completed in 2002, a raised cedar boardwalk leads to three very unusual restrooms. One, called the "tall toilet," rises fifty feet; the "long toilet" is a thirty-foot cantilever; the square "mound toilet" sits on a septic mound. Together with the pavilion, they create what Mayor Edward Daniel of Marion, the Perry County seat, calls "a park nucleus."

The design of the toilets, all of which are wheelchair accessible, was determined by need—the need to create septic mounds—and inventiveness: the students wanted to provide users with three different views. In the tall, topless toilet you look up and see the sky. The long, cantilevered one focuses on a single tree, and the mound toilet has a horizontal slit that provides a broad view of the horizon. An anodized aluminum structure underlies the long and tall toilets, and all are cedar on the inside and stainless steel and cedar on the outside. The contrast between the materials is striking, and the stainless steel, softened by the surroundings woods, reflects the trees.

"We have an opportunity here to make the image or the face of a park," Freear told me in the fall of 2003, "to make a new model for a park, not just let the county show up with cheap facilities and signs. We'll give everybody something they can be very proud of, from toilets to pavilions, to signage, to trails." The studio's successful design for the pavilion convinced the park's governing board to relinquish their initial idea of ordinary prefab toilets. They agreed to go along with the studio's vision of toilets so unusual and grand that people would visit the park just to see them. Daniel says, "What excited me most about this facility is that it's in Perry County, which was considered a third world country. I say to people, this is our Walden Pond."

A boardwalk connects the toilets and the cedar pavilion.

The cantilevered long toilet, with anodized aluminum structure,
is clad in stainless steel and cedar.

Entry to the "mound toilet"

The students wanted to provide distinctive views of the site from
each toilet, so they created a tall enclosure open to the sky, a long
one focused on a single tree, and a square one with a horizontal
slit-opening.

View from the "tall toilet"

View from the "long toilet"

View from the "mound toilet"

NEWBERN LITTLE LEAGUE
BASEBALL FIELD

2003

IT STARTED WITH Joe and Barbara Carlisle, who played sandlot baseball with their sons and daughters and a few neighborhood kids. Soon a handful of youngsters grew to about forty, and Joe formed a team and became its coach. But he could not convince neighboring teams to visit because his ballpark was a rundown open field. "Our goal," Freear says, "was to find the team a home."

Because there was no readily available site, the student architects designed for "a hypothetical one while we searched for land," says team member Jason Hunsucker. Then they made their scheme fit twelve acres that Robert Walthall, a white landowner, offered the black team. The gesture, Freear says "built bridges between the black and white community in Newbern." Serendipitously, the site is next to the Newbern Baseball field, home of the minor league Newbern Tigers and a 2000–01 studio project. Newbern would suddenly have "a sports complex," Freear says, half in jest.

The concept for the backstop evolved from a conventional affair of aluminum poles and chain link into a mittlike curve facing the field and, finally, into metal arches spanned with catfish netting. "Visually, everything disappears but the arches," Hunsucker says. Because the netting is resistant to ultraviolet, it will not dry rot or become degraded by sunlight, and "the beauty of the netting is that everyone in town knows how to fix it," Freear says, alluding to the town's large catfish industry.

The backstop's arches, which enclose all the spectator areas and the dugout, emerge from tubes set into concrete pads four feet below grade. On either side of home plate, where the Little Leaguers sit, the arches are six feet high, scaled for pint-sized viewers. The dugout, also under low arches, is designed so that players cannot see spectators and be distracted by them. The home-team dugout is shaded in the afternoon, while the away team's is in direct sunlight, an intended handicap. In areas where adults congregate—on benches behind home plate and at the concession stand near third base—the arches rise to almost seventeen feet. Another good place for watching games is on the three-and-a-half-foot outfield wall, made of discarded, corrugated, wax-impregnated cardboard bales that cannot be recycled, and, therefore, usually end up in landfills.

The project appeared challenging but not outlandishly difficult, until it was cursed with the wettest winter since 1913. "We'd have to wait six days for the ground to dry, and on the seventh it poured," said team member Julie Hay. The students could not start construction until April 1. And even then rains turned four-foot-deep holes, dug to anchor the arches, into small ponds. The weather added three months to the project. When I visited in May of 2003, it still looked more like a mud field than a baseball field.

Much of the $75,000 budget, including a $25,000 grant from Baseball Tomorrow, went to rent expensive earth-moving equipment to grade the site and improve its drainage. "The money's in the ground; it's not about anything ostentatious," Freear says. The students mounded dirt to divert water from the field and ran three drainage lines, one along each foul line and one along the tree line. The ball field was meant to be a place that even out-of-town teams would proudly have as their home field, Freear says. He thinks the project has "earned the Rural Studio a huge amount of kudos in the community."

The arches are child-sized in the children's seating area and rise
to seventeen feet where adults sit.

The wall above the dugout is made of baled, waste
corrugated cardboard.

The scheme evolved from a conventional backstop into a mittlike curve facing the field, and finally into metal arches spanned with catfish netting.

THOMASTON RURAL HERITAGE CENTER

2003

THE THOMASTON RURAL HERITAGE CENTER won a $190,000 grant from HUD to rehab a big, ugly, 1950s-era building. Originally used for vocational education, the structure would become a showcase for local crafts and a place to make and sell pepper jelly, a specialty of the area. The Rural Studio had to figure out what to do with the building—how to program it—and how to phase the work over a period of years.

If the center's board of directors were not sure what they wanted, they knew what they disliked: the farmer's market, completed by the studio in 2000, that stands in their downtown. Because it was made of unfinished steel, it rusted, and "for these folks rust very much equals decay," Freear says.

The center highlights a number of the changes to the Rural Studio since the days of the farmer's market, some of its problems, and some of the advances it has made. Located about twenty miles south of Newbern, it was a big, complicated project phased over three years. Unlike early studio projects, this one had little of its design done on-site. The new portion was built of steel and glass, so the students ended up spending long hours making precise shop drawings. The result is an immaculately detailed, stunning glazed box. But its steel construction, electrical work, and new roof had to be hired out. The center's architectural vocabulary, unlike that of many early studio works, is minimalist; there are no madcap details or vernacular-based forms and no odd or recycled materials.

One problem the students faced was that they worked inside a building, invisible to the community and deprived of its support. While their classmates were working on the Newbern Little League Baseball Field, neighbors and little leaguers' parents stopped by to offer encouragement and a sense of purpose. But the center's team worked largely in isolation from the community.

Much of their time was consumed with demolition and cleanup. By May of 2003, when the first phase was supposed to be complete, the students had barely started construction. "It was a big site for four people to control," Freear says. They had to knock out bearing walls, put in beams, sandblast old windows—using twelve tons of sand—and add new glazing. Their idea was to literally open the building to visitors.

New construction consisted mainly of inserting a precisely detailed sixteen-by-fifty-foot glass and steel box containing offices, a display wall, and a gift shop. Enclosing these functions in one climate-controlled region spared the center the expense of a large heating and cooling system. The unheated display space around the box serves as an air gap for thermal insulation. The ceiling, though less than eight feet, feels higher because it is transparent. You see through it to the building's twenty-five-foot ceiling. Students call the glass box a ship in a bottle, a bottle in a ship, and even a lifeboat. One side of the glass tube is open office space, the other contains a gift shop, and the end wall is used for displaying jars of pepper jelly.

Once a warren of partitioned spaces, the center is now wide open
and airy.

The glazed end wall elegantly displays jars of pepper jelly, a
local specialty.

Transparency makes the low box appear roomier than its actual size.

EVER-CHANGING, THE RURAL STUDIO REMAINS A MOVING TARGET

THE RURAL STUDIO outreach program underwent a sea change. It began in 2002–03 when John Forney, a trusted critic of the studio, arrived to head the program. During his first year, Cynthia Connolly created an organic vegetable stand with removable gates of hog wire—a patchwork of metal scraps and chicken wire. Lucy Begg made an ingeniously shaded porch addition for an older woman's trailer. Richard Saxton solved the town of York, Alabama's street cleaning problems by rigging together pedicabs with flatbeds. And Garth Brown completed the Bodark Amphitheater on the Rural Studio's grounds, outfitting it with terraced seating and sod.

The 2003 04 outreach participants undertook projects that were socially meaningful and involved no or little construction. Pamela Dorr, a former Gap Corporation executive, teamed up with housing organizations to improve the living situations of Hale County residents. Alex Gilliam, a founder of the Charter High School for Architecture and Design in Philadelphia, introduced a design/build program at Newbern's Sunshine School, where pupils helped upgrade their building He chose five Sunshine youngsters to work on the Newbern fire station, alongside fifth-year Rural Studio students. A high point for the outreach program was the participation of Mockbee's daughter Carol, who began construction of Sub Rosa Pantheon, a meditation building for which Mockbee had made drawings. Carol studied them, divined her father's wishes and intentions, and added her own flourishes.

The academic year 2003–04 was the least tumultuous since Mockbee's death. Freear finally reduced the number of new fifth-year projects, and they were more geographically concentrated. Two were in Newbern: the Patrick House and a fire station that got a slow start and wasn't finished until 2005. Both were thank-yous, in part, to the town for more than ten years of moral support. The downside of working close to home, Freear found, was the neighbors: "If you screw up in Newbern everybody knows about it and has an opinion." Students also got started on the final phase of both the Thomaston Rural Heritage Center and the Perry Lakes Park, the studio's first multistage projects.

In October, the studio's largest exhibition opened at the Birmingham Museum of Art. Freear remembers his lecture on opening night as nerve-wracking, "because all the Rural Studio family was there—the Mockbees and all the people from the beginning. They all knew more than I did."

The year's peak moment occurred in Washington, D.C., on March 3. At the American Architectural Foundation's gala called Accent on Architecture, Julius Mockbee accepted the Gold Medal, the American Institute of Architects' highest honor, on his father's behalf. Samuel Mockbee thus joined Thomas Jefferson, Louis Sullivan, Frank Lloyd Wright, Le Corbusier, Mies van der Rohe, and fifty-four others in a pantheon of architects deemed most worthy by the American architectural profession.

AVERY ORGANIC VEGETABLE STAND

2003

AN OUT-OF-THE-WAY field stands alone off County Road 42, about nineteen miles northeast of Newbern. But everyone within driving distance knew Willie Nell Avery was selling vegetables here even before outreach student Cynthia Connolly built a traffic-stopping stand for her. What catches the eye are the project's sliding gates of hog wire—a weave of pinwheeling license plates and pieces and bits of road signs and an old trailer—created by folk artist Butch Anthony. If you approach when the gates are closed, the vegetable stand looks encased in a colorful collage.

Connolly recalls that she met Anthony, who lives in Seale, Alabama, "when I was batting around the idea for a stand with Willie Nell. Butch's enthusiasm about working on this project was so great that he volunteered to work for free." She was able to pay for some of his time and materials by obtaining small grants from the National Endowment for the Arts and the Alabama Council for the Arts. Connolly, a gregarious artist and photographer, also had help with construction. Friends from Wisconsin helped move earth, poured a concrete floor, set tree trunks as columns, and built the slanting roof. Once Anthony finished welding the sixteen-by-twenty-four-foot frame for the sliding gates, "we had hog wire parties with people pitching in," Connolly says.

Visitors tour the new construction.

At night, light illuminates the gates.

Coming closer, you see old license plates, road signs, and pieces
of old trailers in the hog wire gates.

OLA MAE'S PORCH

2003

THE PROCESS BY WHICH Lucy Begg, a 2002–03 outreach student from London, England, decided to build a new porch for Ola Mae Hill's trailer shows how many small studio projects come about. During her first semester in Newbern, Begg and classmates Cynthia Connolly and Richard Saxton explored western Alabama, met many people, and mentally tested a number of project ideas. Along the way, they became fascinated with the ubiquitous trailer and began wondering if they could help it along. "We got an old trailer donated to us, which we took apart. We had the idea we could make new additions out of old trailers. We met Amos Hill, and he cooked lunch at his house every Friday. So we started hanging out there, eating lunch, and getting to know him. He was enthusiastic about what we were doing, and his sister Ola Mae's trailer was in bad shape. It went from there." Begg says.

She created a screened-in porch addition, big enough for Ola Mae to live in six months of the year, and used materials from the burnt-out trailer for the deck. For summer living she provided various types of shading: she spray painted the screen and built an outrigger with slats that she tied together to form an angled overhang.

Six months of the year, Ola Mae Hill can live in her screened-
porch addition. Its two shed roofs are separated by a clerestory.

To shade the porch, Lucy Begg created slatted, outrigger-type
overhangs and spray painted the screens.

UTILITY NOW! BICYCLE STREET SWEEPERS

2003

THE IDEA FOR this project came to Richard Saxton, a native of Lincoln, Nebraska, after reading a series of articles in the *Birmingham News* that compared west Alabama to a third world country. At the beginning of his year as a Rural Studio outreach student, Saxton, then a Master of Fine Arts candidate at Indiana University, met Mayor Carolyn Mitchell-Gosa of York, Alabama, a town of 2,800 located fifty miles west of Newbern. Before long, Saxton persuaded her that he could help her town with some of its problems. One was basic maintenance of streets. The town had no vehicles for hauling trash, ticketing illegally parked vehicles, or other uses. It bought a mechanical street sweeper in the 1980s, but the machine proved too difficult to operate and maintain. Remembering the *Birmingham News* series, Saxton suggested using a low-tech, low-maintenance vehicle similar to the three-wheeled pedicabs used throughout Asia. The city went for his idea, and he put together two utility tricycles with small flatbeds. One was for the parks and recreation department and the other for the department of public works. He also revamped two regular bicycles, one for each department.

After Saxton completed his year at the studio and received his MFA, the town of York hired him as project director for Utility Now! and as the town's artist-in-residence. In 2003, Saxton built two more tricycles, which gives the city a total of six utility vehicles. During the spring and summer of 2004, he redesigned all six to make them lighter and therefore easier to operate. Saxon has since founded the Municipal Workshop to develop similar solutions for other towns.

Saxton (in sunglasses) and a York employee demonstrate
the project.

BODARK AMPHITHEATER

2003

IN 1996, WILLIAM MORRISETTE donated an 1830s Gothic-revival manse called Chantilly to the Rural Studio and had the house hauled nearly fifteen miles from Greensboro to Newbern. Chantilly remains a renovation waiting to happen, but its formerly flat, scruffy backyard has been transformed into a welcoming amphitheater.

In 2000, thesis students Lee Cooper and Trinity Davis shaped the earth to create a hill sloping down to a flat area where they placed a concrete stage and a metal armature for a canopy. In addition to digging a hole for the stage area, heaping soil from the hole onto the site's west bank, and grading the site into a smooth slope, the partners cut a horizontal slot through the hill and built a retaining wall. As you approach from the west, you climb a grassy hill; the amphitheater does not come into view until you are nearly on top of it.

In 2002–03, Garth Brown, an outreach student, completed the structure. He built terraces into the sloping landscape and topped them with seating made from waste cardboard bales capped with concrete. Then he put in steps and lots of turf. When it was ready for an audience, he worked with neighbors and students from the nearby Sunshine Elementary School to produce two plays; these were performed on the amphitheater's stage as part of the studio's 2003 graduation ceremony. In this remote corner of Alabama, it was the first time in memory that blacks and whites had attended a public, non-sports event together.

PATRICK HOUSE

2004

"GOING INTO THE twelfth year of the Rural Studio, we're certainly having an impact and learning a lot," second-year instructor Jay Sanders told me in the fall of 2003. "But at the end of each year the students and faculty move on, and it all starts over. For us to have a larger impact, we thought we had to do something more important than one project." He and his students decided to create a work that could be duplicated—an easy-to-build, inexpensive alternative to the ubiquitous house trailer. Their solution was to create a steel frame structure that local people could extend, enclose with available materials, and otherwise manipulate to suit themselves.

Sanders, who had worked on the Newbern Baseball Field as a student, wanted the pilot house to be in Newbern. He had made friends in the town and hoped to be more involved with its residents, most of whom "don't really know what we do here. They just know we have a lot of SUVs."

Sanders got permission from the Auburn architecture department to let the community select a client, and he asked Dexter Thornton, a civic leader in Newbern, to choose a client with the help of Thornton's pastor and church members. They selected Willy (Boochie) Patrick, a truck driver who lived with his wife Belle, their seventeen-year-old daughter Kindra, and six-year-old son Willy in a 1950s stick-frame house a few hundred yards beyond Rural Studio's backyard.

The Patricks are not desperately poor, and that led to criticism of the choice, but Sanders wanted to honor Thornton's decision. The Patricks' former home "certainly doesn't lift the spirit," Sanders says. "The square footage is pretty big, but it's been added on to and added on to and airflow and light are very poor. I've heard there's no running water. They don't use the shower there, but rather one at the grandparents' house, behind their house." What cinched the choice for Sanders was the Patrick children. "The experience of working with us has an impact on kids," he says, noting that Richard Bryant, a grandson of Shepard and Alberta Bryant for whom the studio built the Haybale House, is now a college student, the first Bryant to go to college.

During the project's early weeks, Sanders and his students spent time getting to know their clients, mainly by playing dominos—bones, as the game is called locally—with the family outdoors on their property. At the time, the students called their project the Domino House, for the Patricks' favorite pastime and for the project's steel framing, which is reminiscent of architect Le Corbusier's house of the same name. Then the students explored old houses in the area and houses built by the studio and assessed their strengths and deficits. Their discussions evolved from generalities about the rural house as a type to specifics about their clients' needs and way of life. That was when the project became the Patrick House.

Sanders and his first-semester students worked out the house's basic form and elements, its roof and steel frame. They began with a rectangular footprint that yielded 1,000 square feet of space. It would go up in three equal bays and be oriented perpendicular to the old house, which would remain on the site. The Patricks liked to spend time outdoors, and so the students shaped a courtyard that would serve both old and new dwellings. They raised the new house off the ground on footings, having observed that houses that allow air to circulate underneath remain dry during storms. Sanders and the students likened the shape of the house to an African-American woman with high-heeled shoes and a big hat.

The easiest roof form would have been a continuous shed or gable, but Sanders and the students decided on a combination shed and gable to satisfy the students' wish to do something different. From the north, it looks like a butterfly roof, but it consists of two shed roofs slanting in opposite directions that meet at the center of the house in a gable.

The students placed the parents' bedroom and bath on the ground floor of the south bay, close to the old house, and Kindra's loft above her parents' room. The living area and a loft for the younger Willy are in the north bay, and the middle bay has the kitchen, which overlooks the living area. Glazed doors open to the courtyard.

The first-semester students left the question of how to fill in the steel frame to their successors, thinking they would use wood pallets, hay bales, surplus cardboard, carpet tile, or some other leftover material. "We thought in terms of scrapping the house altogether," Sanders said. His inspiration came, in part, from Charley Lucas, a folk artist from Selma known as Tin Man, who worked at the Rural Studio during the fall of 2003 and had built his house from wood palettes and scrap tin.

But second-semester students tend to approach a design as though reinventing it, Sanders says, and in this instance they abandoned the idea of enclosing the steel structure with unconventional materials. Their priority was to finish the project on schedule and within the original budget, so they decided to buy standard wall construction lumber from Lowe's. As exterior cladding they used one-by-six-inch boards, applied horizontally, to achieve an effect similar to that of the interior of the Butterfly House's porch, where an occasional white board animates the architecture.

To open the house, the students put twin eight-foot-high glass doors on either side of the central bay and lots of donated Pella windows elsewhere. Each loft has its own stairs, and Willy's loft has a porthole window. The students walled some interior spaces with exterior cladding material.

You may wonder, what about the Patricks' old house? "That's up to them," Sanders replies.

155

The new Rural Studio project stands next to the Patricks'
former home.

Living room and kitchen, with glazed doors that open to the
courtyard

Willy Patrick looks up to his loft bedroom

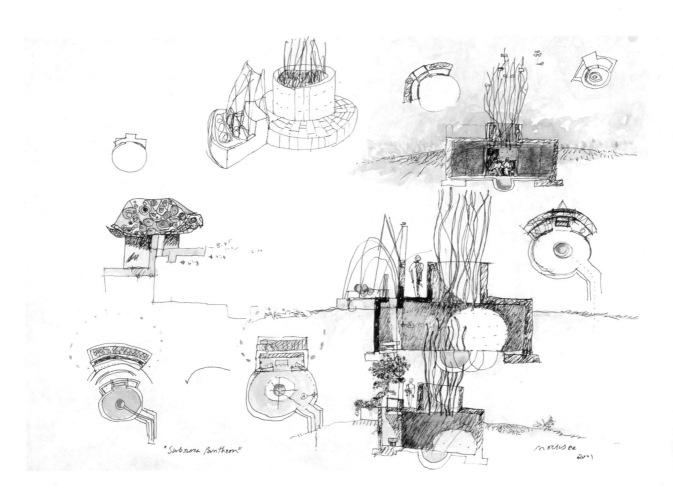

Samuel Mockbee, *Sub Rosa Pantheon*, 2001

"Subrosa Pantheon"

mockbee
2001

EXPERIENCING THE RURAL STUDIO

INTERVIEWS WITH STUDENTS, A TEACHER, AND A CLIENT

CAROL MOCKBEE
OUTREACH STUDENT, 2003–

Carol Mockbee, the youngest of Sambo and Jackie Mockbee's three daughters—and older sister to their son Julius—was twenty years old when her father died. "As a child," she says, "I never thought about the fact that my father was an artist and was cool and that he was doing great things for other people. In high school I began to catch on a little. A lot of people in town thought he was weird: he was this big mountain man with a beard, outside in the summers doing art. I never thought it was weird. He was always too much fun. I thought we were normal and everyone else was different. It was just how we grew up." Her father began taking her to the studio, mainly for special events, when she was twelve. "I grew up around the students, the professors, and the people who live around here, but there was a huge part of the Rural Studio that I didn't know, and a huge part of my father that I didn't know," Carol told me.

When Carol was twenty-two, she decided to become an outreach student and finish a project begun by her father. She wanted to know him as an adult. Since his death, she said, nothing has excited her as much as the prospect of being at the studio and finishing a project for which her father had made drawings. "It's a way to continue learning from him," she said.

Together with other outreach students, Carol began her first semester in September 2003 doing "neck-down" work,

the studio's term for grunt work. It engages students in the community before they settle into individual projects. Each fall, Ann Langford, the studio's administrative assistant, gets a list from her church of people in the area needing home repairs and passes the list to the students. "We went to see which projects we could actually do, which ones were too big," Carol said. "There is a lady near Sawyerville who is diabetic, and her back porch was falling in. So we went out there, knocked on her door, and she was as welcoming as could be. In three days, we tore down her porch and built a new one. We also fixed a railing for a young man in a wheelchair. These projects are huge for the family. They're real contributions. They make you unafraid of going out and talking to people or asking if they need something. They make you realize you can do so much, and they make you less afraid of designing."

After completing this neck-down work, Carol focused on her main project. In 1999 her father made drawings for a project he called "Sub Rosa Pantheon" (see examples at left and on the following page) to be located on the studio's campus behind the Bodark Amphitheater. Carol is interpreting her father's drawings of Sub Rosa and building it. Explaining the name, Carol said, "When we were growing up and my parents told us something was *sub rosa*, we knew we couldn't repeat it. I've grown up with the term meaning: hold the secret or die." The word derives from the fact that the ancient Romans would hang roses or plaster casts of roses over important and confidential meetings. The rose was a symbol for the Holy Grail and was closely tied to the concept of true direction; the compass rose helped travelers navigate, as did rose lines, the longitudinal lines on maps. The rose speaks of secrecy, womanhood, and guidance, all of which may be important in Carol Mockbee's current quest.

Sambo Mockbee's drawings show a kiva-like structure—circular, a few feet below grade, partially open to the sky, and approached through a tunnel. At the bottom is a pond for two Black Warrior River turtles, major players in his mythology. Carol recalls asking him the meaning of the turtle in one of his paintings. "It's whatever you want it to mean. You'll figure it out," her father told her. His drawings show roses on tall beaver sticks or steel supports emerging from the turtle pond. There is a bench in Sub Rosa and one above it, between which

Samuel Mockbee, *Sub Rosa Pantheon*, 2001

secrets can be whispered through a tube. Key to the project, Carol explains, will be drainage to prevent the turtle pool from overflowing after heavy rains.

Carol spent many hours researching the meanings of *sub rosa*, studying her father's sketchbooks, and trying to understand his readings in astronomy that had increasingly influenced his view of the project. "I can look through some of his books, and it's like he's pointing things out to me. I know what he's thinking sometimes, so it's really exciting. Yes, I feel like he's sitting on my shoulder." She added that she could also "feel him here, through Jay, Andrew, Johnny, and the others. Things Andrew will say, the way he runs things, the way he wants us to do things—all remind me of my father."

Is Sub Rosa a memorial to her father? "It is, definitely, to me," she said. "It's a mystical meditation space, but it's meant for whatever you want it to be." I suggested to Carol, who still became teary when talking about her father, that

confronting him daily and honestly showed bravery. "I think it's brave too," she said. "I am looking right at him. Sambo would say, 'Bring it on. Proceed and be bold.' That's what you gotta do. I'm trying."

Her college major was interior design. Is that what she wants for a career? "I want to go to architecture school," she answered. "At least that's how I'm thinking now. If you're an architect, you can design, you can build. You're a carpenter and an artist. An architect is the best profession anyone could ever have. You can be whatever you want to be if you're an architect. My father was everything—an artist, an adventurer, an environmentalist—and he was an architect."

She continued, "You find out a lot of things about yourself out here. Every day I'm learning about how I react to things. I'm learning about the building process. I can't imagine how different I'll be when I leave, certainly more knowledgeable about design and engineering and construction. It's already happening."

162

MARI MICHAEL GLASSELL
SECOND-YEAR STUDENT, 2003–04

Mari Michael Glassell grew up in the small resort community of Gulf Shores, Alabama. "I've never experienced the kind of poverty I'm experiencing in Hale County," she told me in late 2003 during a break from her work on the Patrick House. What impressed her most about the people she met in Newbern was that they have "so much heart. I've talked to a lot of people, especially to the domino gang, the Patricks. I played dominos with them. Often, people just sit on their porches and wave to us as we walk by. They're real welcoming. Everybody eats catfish at the baseball games together and knows everybody; everybody goes to G.B. Mercantile and sits on its porch talking. Henry Reed, across the street from G.B.'s, is usually on his porch, and I go talk to him. There's more trust and friendship here than I've seen in Gulf Shores. I think I'll take that away with me."

Why did she come to the studio? "In architecture school, you can design and draw, but you don't have to worry about how to level the ground, and you don't get to experience clients," she explained. "Here we're designing for real people. It makes me feel as though what I'm doing has real purpose."

A surprise, she said, was "how you really learn to trust each other. At architecture school, you're used to doing everything by yourself. Here, you start to learn how to work together. You learn that people have different strengths,

and you work with it. That's what happens in the real world." At the beginning of the semester, "people were shy about expressing their opinions or taking ownership of ideas. They're starting to realize their strength. Students are becoming more down-to-earth. We're learning to know when people are in bad moods and how to handle it." She was impressed with "how doing architecture can help us grow and mature."

At the Rural Studio, Glassell has learned some building process basics, "how building elements go together, how to support roofs and floor joists," she said. And she has become more familiar with materials. Her group experimented with milk crates and shipping pallets as cladding, and "how you can get the same effects from salvaged as from bought materials. We're learning about different insulation values of different materials." Did she intend to return for her fifth year? "Definitely," she answered. "The Rural Studio has been the best experience of my architectural career."

JULIE HAY
SECOND-YEAR STUDENT, 1999–2000
FIFTH-YEAR STUDENT, 2002–03

When I met Julie Hay, she was seventeen feet off the ground and bent over one of the steel arches of the recently completed Newbern Little League Baseball Field, her thesis project. After she finished mending a piece of catfish netting that spans the backstop's arches, she stepped onto the arm of a backhoe, was lowered back to earth, and joined me for a talk. It was five months after her graduation. Bad weather had delayed her project, making it trail into the summer and early fall. The field had been dedicated just days before my visit in October 2003. "The little leaguers' whole families came," she said. "There were four- and five-year-old brothers and sisters climbing on the net, falling down, scrambling back up, swinging. I think they had the most fun. The whole community came, maybe a hundred people. Some were sitting on the outfield wall; the concessions sold Boston butt ribs and catfish, candy bars, cokes."

She recalled that when she was assigned to the baseball field, it was her last choice among the available projects. "I thought, ho hum, a baseball field: they already have a baseball field. I didn't see the need for it until I got to know what it was really about. We've given kids in Hale County a place where they can play ball and grow up, where they can be safe, make friends, and learn teamwork and commitment."

Baseball is especially important to these children, she said, because Coach Joe Carlisle is such a father figure to them; "When they get report cards, they run and tell Joe."

She recognized that even bad weather and disagreements among her three Rural Studio teammates offered lessons. "We went through a really hard time," she said. "At the beginning, we didn't have a site and felt like maybe nobody wanted to help us; we'd been searching and searching and getting nowhere. When the Walthall family stepped up with a donation of land, it was still uphill for a while. It rained. Amazing how much it rained. We dug four-foot holes for our arches and had the formwork set up to pour concrete the next day. That night it rained and filled the holes with mud and silt. Our team also got into heated arguments, but we stuck it through, got over it, and, as Andrew says, we built trust among us. I realize now how close the Rural Studio community is. I feel a part of it, which is gratifying. I think I wasn't expecting that when I came out thesis year."

The product of a private-school education in Huntsville, a relatively affluent north Alabama aerospace center, Hay says that before coming to the Rural Studio, she "assumed that most communities were like my hometown and that hometowns could provide for their residents." She spent a semester of her second year at the studio and "became a part of the culture," she said, "which educated me about poverty and made it more personal." One of her misconceptions, she said, was thinking that poor people do not have strong families. "Now I know how wrong that is, because I got to know parents and grandparents."

Comparing her fifth year at the studio with her second year, she says that, for her, the second time around was a richer experience because she worked with a smaller group and saw her project through from start to finish. "The four of us became very, very close, working together day and night for a year. As thesis students, you live and breathe your project; the project becomes your life. Every member of my team spent hours researching different construction details, not because it was required but because we wanted everything designed and constructed really well. None of us will ever leave the baseball field experience behind."

JAY SANDERS
SECOND-YEAR STUDENT, 1997–98
FIFTH-YEAR STUDENT, 2000–01
CLERK OF WORKS, 2001–02
SECOND-YEAR INSTRUCTOR, 2002–04

The high point of Jay Sanders's two-year teaching career was getting to know Music Man, a.k.a., Jimmy Lee Matthews, for whom Sanders and his students built a house. His friendship with Music Man, Sanders told me, "was my first serious relationship with someone living in poverty." When they met, Music Man was living in a rusty trailer without running water or heat. "Here was someone living in such bad conditions, but his spirit was just so amazing," Sanders said. "It made me and my students feel like we didn't know anything. We all felt that Music Man did a better job of living on this planet than we did. It changed our outlook."

The secret to getting the most from being at the Rural Studio and building well, he said, is to immerse yourself in the place and get to know its people. "You have to earn respect, and the way to do that is to meet as many people and do as many things as possible, with your head up, your best

manners, and your best handshake." Asked what he wanted his second-year students to take away from their Rural Studio experience, Sanders said, "There's so much young architects are capable of doing to better the world or improve the lives of others. I think they can realize here that college is about learning what they can do, not about getting a better job."

He added, "Sambo said that to have an impact on architecture and architectural education, maybe he'd have to go straight to the students. Maybe the students will have to make the needed changes in the profession, because the academics and architects are not going to try anything exciting." Like Mockbee, Sanders puts faith in students. He said, "It took a lot of guts on Sambo's part to bet people's well-being on young people with very little architectural training. But they make the right decisions because they care about those families."

A Fort Worth native, Sanders never followed the pack. He decided to enroll at Auburn in 1996 "because all my friends were going to Texas Tech," he said. "I wanted to do something different." But Auburn's architecture school left him hungry. He skated through his early classes, he said, by knowing how to draw a little and make presentations. But because there was nothing at stake, it was "more of an artistic endeavor than anything else," and he was not excited about being a conventional architect. "I had this horrible feeling that it wasn't what I wanted to do. I was determined not to be a CAD jockey."

When he spent spring semester of his second year at the Rural Studio, he says, he "was snake bit" by Mockbee's magic plus the allure of Hale County. At the studio he learned basic things about materials and construction, and he enjoyed "being in a unique community." Extroverted and energetic, he steeped himself in the place. He played baseball with the Newbern club, got to know its African-American players, and decided he wanted to return fifth year to upgrade their seventy-year-old playing field.

As a thesis student in 2000–01, he and two classmates "walked right up to Major Ward, the manager of the team, and asked him if we could build him a new backstop," Sanders said. He recalled that "we began to have community meetings, though rarely more than five people attended, including Major Ward; Eddie Smith, the fifty-five-year-old pitcher/treasurer; Melvin Rox, who sells scrapple at the games and mows the field; and Washington Turner, an ex-player who wears his old jersey while collecting admissions at the gate. We heard stories about Bubba Page, an outfielder who did a stint in the New York Mets farm system. We interviewed T. J. Johnson, a left-handed pitcher who played for the Cincinnati Reds organization after playing here, and we took the regulars on a tour of other Rural Studio projects."

During his fifth year Sanders also launched the Beacon Street Gallery in a rented warehouse in Greensboro. He held art exhibits for local talent at the gallery, converted two small rooms in the building into apartments for himself and a friend, and obtained a grant from the Alabama Arts Commission for Beacon Street artists to teach art to elementary school students in Newbern.

One day at the end of his studies, Sanders read a magazine interview in which "Sambo talked about wanting to have interns come to the Rural Studio. I found him that day," Sanders said, "and told him I'd be an intern if he let me, for free." Mockbee created a jack-of-all-trades position, clerk of works, so that Sanders could help him with preliminary construction on the Sub Rosa Pantheon. Sanders also worked on the Bodark Amphitheater and the Rural Studio exhibit at New York's Whitney Museum Biennial of 2002.

During Mockbee's last afternoon at the studio, in December 2001, having just been diagnosed with pneumonia and planning to check himself into the hospital the next morning, he drafted and signed paperwork ensuring that Sanders would be the second-year instructor the following fall. Mockbee, who tended to heap responsibility on talented people even when they had little or no experience, was confident that the twenty-four-year-old would learn to teach on the job. Mockbee suggested Sanders limit his teaching stint to two years, because he was wary of burnout.

Sanders honored his agreement with Mockbee and left in the Spring of 2004, despite being as energized and eager as when he began teaching in September 2002. "I can't think of anything better to do with my time," he told me. "I like every part of being here. I like driving around Hale County. I like the people. I like building. I like thinking about our projects."

In the Fall of 2004, Sanders entered the Master of Fine Arts program at the University of Texas at Austin. Now, he said, "I think it's my responsibility to take part of what I learned outside of Hale County. I need to reflect on what I've learned here, test it, and be inspired by someone or something new."

EDWARD DANIEL

MAYOR OF MARION, ALABAMA, 1996–
CLIENT, 2001–04

Edward Daniel has compared Perry Lakes Park to Walden
Pond. "What excited me most about this facility is that it's in
Perry County, which was considered a third world country,"
he told me in January 2004. At the time he was serving
his second term as mayor of Marion, the county seat, and was
a member of the governing board of Perry Lakes Park. The
board has served as the Rural Studio's client on a three-year
project for the park that was two-thirds complete when Daniel
and I talked. The first phase of design and construction
produced a pavilion, with a shimmering stainless steel roof,
that is used for family reunions and other outdoor events.
Then the studio built three eye-catching restrooms—each
clad in stainless steel and cedar, and each a different shape—
and a raised boardwalk connecting them to the pavilion. The
third phase, in construction in mid-2004, consists of signage
and a bridge spanning an oxbow.

The most daunting part of the work, said Daniel, was the
process of getting the park reopened after it was closed
during the 1970s. The U.S. Department of the Interior and
the Alabama Department of Conservation and Natural
Resources shared ownership of the land, Daniel said. "We
could not cut through the red tape, because the feds and the
state had conflicting interests." What finally broke the logjam
was a bill introduced by U.S. Senator Richard Shelby of
Alabama and signed by President Bill Clinton in 2000 that
deeded six hundred acres to the state.

The relationship between the Perry Lakes Park governing
board and the Rural Studio was a natural, according to Daniel.
The board knew of the studio's work in neighboring Hale
County. It also knew that using a commercial contractor to
design and build facilities for the park would have been
prohibitively expensive and probably very time-consuming.
"The Rural Studio offered not only to design and build what
we needed, but they also got some materials donated. It's
hard to turn that down," he said.

"I don't think the process could have gone smoother,"
Daniel continued. "When the students brought up the idea of
a pavilion, we believed it was just going to be a run-of-the-
mill A-frame, not thinking that these young designers
would have such bright ideas." He said the students started
by "drawing and drawing and drawing, and they'd bring
drawings to our board meetings. We were tickled pink; the
pavilion gave us a heck of a lift. It's one of the brightest things
that has happened in Perry County in a long time."

Daniel said he visited the construction site weekly "as an
encouragement," and got to know the students. Asked if
he thought they were sincere in their concern for the county
and its people, he said, "Absolutely. They had to be sincere.
Not being seasoned contractors, they found the work difficult.
They were there from day one, either sawing or hammering
or drilling or digging. And lots of times they worked until
nightfall and on weekends. You wouldn't dream of taking on a
task like that without being sincere." Besides, he said, they
returned after graduation to finish their projects, when they
could have gone on and got paying jobs. "I commend them for
staying the course."

What did he learn from being a client? "It's easier now
for me to judge and evaluate drawings," he said. "I learned to
respect how artistic some people can be. I especially learned
to appreciate things that are different from what we expect."

BUILDING A PAVILION

Jennifer Bonner

THE FIRST TIME our team—Nathan Orrison, Anthony Tindill, Mary Beth Maness, and I—explored our thesis site, we crept out onto a flooding landscape caused by a change in course by the winding Cahaba River. This was the old Perry Lakes Park, which was created in the 1930s by the Works Progress Administration and closed in the 1970s. Left behind was a place that had been untouched by the people of Perry County for over thirty years. The lake had deeply rooted cypress trees and water tupelos twisting and turning out of its murky water, while Spanish moss hung from the branches and nests made by blue herons towered over us. The land was densely overgrown and later revealed itself to us as remarkably mysterious.

Perry County is the poorest county in Alabama. Probate Judge Donald Cook realized there was a need in his county for a place where people could picnic, fish, learn, canoe, enjoy, and grow as a community. For twelve years, beginning in 1990, he wrote grant proposals to raise money for the park. When our team heard of his work in late August 2001, we went to meet with him and to express our interest in helping him with this project. He shared his vision with us, and on that day a working relationship between Perry County and the Rural Studio began.

As a team, we four committed to design/build for the people of Perry County a pavilion to serve as a community center, an outdoor classroom for a local college and schools, a place for family reunions, and, ultimately, a civic destination. A governing board of community leaders was formed and its members served as our clients. In addition to Judge Cook, the board consisted of Edward Daniel, Mayor of Marion, the Perry County seat; Johnny Flowers, the county commissioner; Maurice Jackson, manager of the Marion state fish hatcheries; Milford Smith, a representative of Alabama Power; and Keith Tassin, a member of the Nature Conservancy of Alabama. The advisors to the board were Thomas Wilson, head of the biology department at Judson College, and Bill Dean, county engineer.

Throughout the design and construction phases of the project, we met with our clients every two weeks, whether to discuss budget issues, give a formal presentation of our ideas, or informally explain what we had accomplished since we last met. We quickly learned that holding the meetings on site

made it easier for us to explain our ideas and for the board to make decisions and express opinions. For weeks, which turned into months, we showed them models, drawings, and mock-ups of our proposals. Each step of the way they appeared to have complete confidence in us, always cheering us on.

We began our research by exploring every acre of the site. We hiked. We canoed the Cahaba River and the oxbow lake. We camped. We numbered and tagged the 109 trees in the old picnic area, then transferred the data into drawings and site models. We collected specimens or objects we found on the site that interested us and placed them into mason jars. This exercise was extremely helpful at the beginning of the project, because the site and the scope of work seemed vast and overwhelming. Along with exploring and collecting, we invited local birdwatchers, entomologists, and biologists to help us as we learned about the site. We made it a priority to be at the site every day, twenty-five miles away from Newbern, regardless of the weather. We immersed ourselves in the place.

Once we became familiar with the site and had met with our clients many times, we retreated to our studio in Newbern to begin drawing. We sketched in our individual sketchbooks, making photocopies for each team member, and then sat down and talked about our ideas. We would take the copies, sketch over them, and discuss what they meant. We called it "getting our dreams out." We did this exercise every day for two weeks. We made a series of study models and site models.

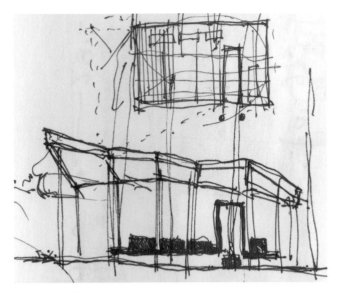
Plan and elevation

We composed a set of construction drawings, using AutoCAD. We worked alone, we worked in pairs, and eventually we worked as a team of four designers.

After desk critiques with our thesis professor, Andrew Freear, and Sambo Mockbee, formal juries with visiting Auburn professors, and presentations to our clients, we began to solidify a design for the pavilion. Site placement was a crucial decision and an issue of debate among us. Therefore, we decided to construct a life-size study model on the site.

We discovered an area that was tucked into the trees, spilled out into the picnic area, and faced the oxbow lake in the distance. We found large rolls of canvas in an old barn in Newbern, took them to the site, and hung them from the trees to mimic the roof. We learned how light filtered through the canvas and saw how the leaves peeked into the covered space. The installation allowed us to gain a true sense of scale, proportion, height, and space in our vast landscape. The hanging canvases also convinced us that we wanted the roof to appear as though it was floating in the air as one came upon it from the forest. Making a model on the site, then standing and sitting underneath the space it created, helped us envision the pavilion that we would soon build.

From the beginning, we wanted the community to be involved in our project, so we wrote an article in the *Marion Times* asking for donated materials. A few weeks later, we received a phone call from Mary Ward Brown, a short story writer who became a close friend. She offered to donate a cedar grove on her property for the project.

Cedar does well when wet, and our board constantly reminded us that we were building in a flood plane. Without proper flood maps of the county, we relied heavily on recollections by local people. We learned all we could about cedar. We harvested the trees ourselves and worked closely with Robby Lindsey, who milled the lumber for us on his portable sawmill. We challenged ourselves to test and then use the cedar trees in every way possible. In the end, we used cedar as the floor finish; cedar scraps to line the inside of the formwork to texture the concrete footings; and cedar chips underneath the deck to act as a natural mosquito repellent. Cedar is the project's principal material.

Near the end of January, we began surveying and stringing off the footings at the site, then devoted a month to site work and foundations. We sited the pavilion so that we did not have to cut down trees, but they closely surround the space. A local machine shop fabricated steel columns according to our construction drawings. Once the columns were erected, we lifted the glue-laminated beams into place and secured them with a simple pin connection. This was a crucial day for each of us as it was March 15 and the thought of graduating in six weeks closed in on us. After this moment, there was a steady hum of the generator accompanying us as we continued working each day, sun up to sun down. We began by framing the roof. Each two-by-six-inch rafter had to have custom angles due to the drastic incline and change of pitch in the roof plane from beam to beam. So each rafter had to be measured, cut, labeled, and secured into place one at a time.

After we constructed the roof, it protected us from the hot Alabama sun as we began building the deck. It is a pristine, floating floor plane that is raised eighteen inches from the ground. This allows the deck to act as one large seat. The deck wraps up to form benches and wraps up again, as a bold gesture, to make a formal entrance into the pavilion. The entrance is enclosed with cedar on either side and contains

Students hung strips of canvas from the trees to work out ideas for a roof.

project rich because they reveal layers of thought rather than hasty solutions. In the end, the details tell the story of how the pavilion stands boldly yet quietly in the landscape.

A year after the pavilion's completion, I had the opportunity to observe it regularly in its changing landscape. Sometimes it was quiet as it sat tucked in the woods; the only noise we heard was our feet treading over the ground and the sounds of the wildlife around us. Sometimes it was filled with people, frying catfish, with a full spread of food laid out over the deck. Sometimes it was used as an outdoor classroom. The pavilion's form took the shape of a megaphone, announcing the activity and life of fourth-grade children filling out their science worksheets. And then, finally, after discussing the possibility of a flood for an entire year, it happened! We waded out in the deep water and stood in front of the pavilion as the water crept up to the deck's edge, but no further.

Now, as the four of us begin our professional careers and scatter throughout the world, we each take away invaluable knowledge, memories, and insight. All of this cannot be said without acknowledging the struggles we faced each day as we learned how to compromise. We grew as we communicated as a team. Many aspects of our experience are very hard to describe or adequately express, but what can be said is that the design/build experience offered us an educational opportunity to make real decisions, take responsibility, and provide a service to others. But this process and the Rural Studio is much more than making architecture, it is about deeply investing ourselves in a community that will forever be in our minds.

a handicapped-accessible ramp. We occasionally refer to the entrance as the "box," not only because of its form, but also because it turns into an aromatic cedar box.

The pavilion has two main spaces—a large gathering space that spills out into the landscape and a small intimate area tucked behind the entrance, where we designed a "kissing bench" for two to sit and watch the sunset. The columns seem to disappear in the trees as they hold the hovering roof plane that dances overhead.

As a team, we realized from the beginning that each of us would have to stand firmly behind decisions we made about the project's details. Detailing asks that careful attention be given to small decisions. It is not just a matter of connections, but also a matter of totality—not just making the pieces fit, but making them harmonize as they tie together and seal a building. Details take time. They make a

Patrick McFarlin, *Samuel Mockbee*, part of portrait series at the Birmingham Museum of Art, 2001

ANOTHER DIMENSION OF SAMBO

Jackie Mockbee

MY FAMILY AND I were excited to be at the National Building Museum to accept the 2004 AIA Gold Medal Award for Sambo on March 3, 2004. Sambo would have been honored to share the podium with I. M. Pei, who most deservedly won the AIA's Twenty-five Year Award for his East Building of the National Gallery of Art, and with Lake/Flato, who were given the AIA Firm Award.

Sambo worked a long, long time to achieve all that he did. He decided that he wanted to be an architect when he was six years old. He would sit with his mother at her dining room table and draw floor plans and design buildings. There is still an imprint of a church on his mother's mahogany table. She loved it. At the age of twenty-nine, fresh out of Auburn, Sambo made another conscious decision that would guide his career for the next twenty-eight years. He promised himself that he would make great architecture.

At the heart of all this was Sambo's sincere care for others. He started that at a young age, too. He entertained the neighborhood kids with every game and project imaginable, from fallout shelters and pony rides to kick the can and capture the flag. When he was in the army and returned home for a weekend, the neighborhood children would come and knock on the door and ask if Sambo could come out and play.

Sambo lived the life he presented to others. He noticed people—really looked at them and listened, saw their needs, and tried to get everyone involved to help make a difference. Along the way, he touched so many lives—there is no way to count them all, but we feel this influence daily. We hear from someone, run into someone, read an article or get a phone call. Grown men and women, whom we have never met, called our home and cried when they heard that he had died. His legacy will live on because good things do not go away.

Now, I would like to tell you about what meant the most to Sambo: our children and I. There was never a doubt in any of our minds that we were what was most important in his life. When our children were infants, Sambo would place them on his chest to sleep while he took his powernaps. As they got older and heard him walk in the door, they all went running to see who could get to him first. He walked down the hall with one child holding onto each foot, one on his back, and one in his arms. While he painted in his art shed, he would make sure everyone had contributed at least a stroke or two. He never said, "I'm tired." He never said, "Not now." It was *always* about us. So now, I would like you to know who our children are.

Margaret is our first born. She is an attorney practicing in Athens, Georgia. She and her husband Robby Luckett married in May 2004.

Sarah Ann is our middle daughter. She graduated from Barnard College, majoring in English, in June 2003. She and her husband Sam Douglas were married the following fall.

Carol is our baby daughter. She is a recent graduate of Auburn University with a degree in Interior Design. She is currently an outreach fellow at the Rural Studio working on a project Sambo started, the Sub Rosa Pantheon. Sambo said this was the most important project of his career. In 1999 he began drawings, and shortly thereafter work on the project started. Carol has picked up where he left off, adding some of her own ideas, and will complete the project her father began.

Julius is our son. He is a junior at Maplebrook High School in Amenia, New York, and will graduate in May 2005. He is interested in computers and hopes to go to school in this field.

When our children were young and we would tuck them into bed, Sambo would slip them Oreo cookies after I made sure they had brushed their teeth. He encouraged each one to be respectful of others but to never follow the rules too closely. Sambo led by example and I see him in each of our children. Margaret's determination, Sarah Ann's thoughtfulness, Carol's independence, and Julius's smile embody the best parts of him, and I am grateful every time I see the influence he continues to have on each of them.

PROJECT CREDITS

AKRON SENIOR CENTER, 2002
Instructor: Andrew Freear
Matthew A. Barrett, Jonathan Winston Graves, Breanna N. Hinderliter, Joseph A. Yeager

ANTIOCH BAPTIST CHURCH, 2002
Instructor: Andrew Freear
Jared Dwight Fulton, Marion Elizabeth McElroy, Gabriel T. Michaud, William K. Nauck

HERO STOREFRONT, 2002
Instructor: Andrew Freear
John Michael McCabe, Andrea Ray, Daniel L. Sweeney, R. Matt Wilson

LUCY'S HOUSE, 2002
Instructors: Samuel Mockbee and D. K. Ruth
Floris Keverling Buisman, Ben Cannard, Philip Michael Crosscup, Kerry J. Larkin, Marie Richard, James Michael Tate, Keith Zawistowski

PERRY LAKES PARK PAVILION, 2002
Instructor: Andrew Freear
Jennifer Rae Bonner, Mary Beth Maness, Nathan Robert Orrison, Anthony T. Tindill

ROOM FOR ESSIE AND JAB, 2002
Instructor: Andrew Freear
Jody W. Touchstone

SHILES HOUSE, 2002
Instructor: Steve Hoffman
Carl Dereck Aplin, Joshua Paul Arnett, Erin Rebecca Aubry, Robert Jackson Austin, Glen Allen Barfield, Amy Kathryn Holer Bell, Adrienne C. Brady, Laura C. Filipek, John Hunter Foshee, Jonathan Kent Fuller, David E. Garner, Amy Marie Green, Amanda Leigh Herron, Paul B. Howard, Angela Leigh Hughey, Gabriel Ika, Carrie E. Jaxon, Shawn Lee Kent, Catherine Ann Liscum, Stephen F. Long, Janice Patricia Madden, Elise Nicole McDermott, Gary Robert Miller, Jr. Coley Martin Mulcahy, Leslie Alyson Myers, Amy Tera Owen, Brian Chance Parrish, Scott Pickens, James C. Rutherford, Katherine V. Scott, Manley Lamarr Seale, Turnley Hall Smith, Monica Brown Starling, Alan Keeth Stevenson, Samuel Lee Vines, Lauren Willson

AVERY ORGANIC VEGETABLE STAND, 2003
Instructor: John Forney
Cynthia Connolly

BODARK AMPHITHEATER, 2003
Instructor: James Forney
Thornton Garth Brown

LEE COUNTY AIDS ALABAMA HOUSE, 2003
Instructor: D. K. Ruth
Travis Burke, Erik Ayers Lindholm, Seth P. Rodwell, Jason Schmidt

MUSIC MAN'S HOUSE, 2003
Instructor: Jay Sanders
John W. Ayers, David Carl Boettcher, Blair Forres Bricken, Julieta V. Collart, Benjamin L. Collins, David J. Davis, Leigh Ann Duncan, Lana Elizabeth Farkas, Robert Connely Farr, John N. Foust, L. Tate Foy, Lauren Avery Frayer, Alicia Johan Gjesvold, Nicholas Wayne Gray, Philip M. Hamilton, Chang Yub Kim, Allison C. Kulpa, Jonathan M. Mahorney, Mary Helen Neal, Mona B. Pedro, Jeremy Daryl Sargent, Heidi Ann Schattin, Dustin Shue, Daniel Rob Splaingard, Jennifer Thompson, Lillian M. Ulmer, Ryan D. Vernon, Tamika L. Watts, Mark D. Wise, Robert Holcomb Wright, Joseph M. Yester, Jessica Florence Zenor

NEWBERN LITTLE LEAGUE BASEBALL FIELD, 2003
Instructor: Andrew Freear
Julie Corinne Hay, Jason Andrew Hunsucker, Richard Patrick Nelson, Jermaine Washington

OLA MAE'S PORCH, 2003
Instructor: John Forney
Lucy Begg

PERRY LAKES PARK FACILITIES, 2003
Instructor: Andrew Freear
Sarah Elizabeth Dunn, Daniel Matthew Foley, Brannen L. Park,
Melissa M. Sullivan

RED BARN, 2003
Instructor: Andrew Freear
Andrew Freear, Johnny Parker, Alfred (A.J.) Jordan, Lerone
(Big Selma) Smiley

THOMASTON RURAL HERITAGE CENTER, Phase 1, 2003
Instructor: Andrew Freear
Kathryn Elizabeth Bryan, John David Caldwell, Emily Marie
McGlohn, William Walker Renneker

UTILITY NOW! BICYCLE STREET SWEEPERS, 2003
Instructor: John Forney
Richard Saxton

PATRICK HOUSE, 2004
Instructor: Jay Sanders
Joe William Aplin, Lindsay Eleanor Butler, Robert D.
Callighan, Elizabeth Ann Clayton, Samantha Lynn Coffey,
Laura Beth Daniel, Russell Benjamin Gibbs, Jennifer Grace
Givens, Marilyn (Mari Michael) Glassell, Bonnie K. Gorman,
Whitney L. Hall, Virginia Frances Hammock, Shelly E. Martin,
John Thomas Marusich, Walter Gunter Mason, Adam J.
Pearce, Emily Hayden Phillips, Pamela Lynn Raetz, Willaundia
D. Reddo, Thomas Joseph Russell, Melissa Renee Schricker,
Evelyn-Pierce Butler Smith, Joseph Raleigh Sullivan, Emily
Wilde Tanner, Robin Elaine Virga, Anthony Tran Vu, Adam S.
Woodward

GREAT HALL IMPROVEMENTS, 2004
Instructor: John Forney and Andrew Freear
Matthew Christopher, Clark Todd Gollotte, Kristopher Heath
Johnson, Daniel B. McHugh, Albert Ulease Mitchum, II

GOVERNMENT HOUSING ASSISTANCE, 2004
Instructor: John Forney
Pamela Dorr

NEWBERN FIRE STATION, 2004
Instructor: Andrew Freear
William C. Brothers, Elizabeth Ellington, Matthew T. Finley,
Leia W. Price

OUTSIDE IN, 2004
Instructor: John Forney
Emily K. Chaffee

PERRY LAKES PARK SIGNAGE AND BRIDGE, 2004
Instructor: Andrew Freear
Matthew W. Edwards, Lynielle J. Houston, Charles T.
Jorgensen, Sara B. Singleton

SUB ROSA PANTHEON, 2004
Instructor: John Forney
Carol C. Mockbee

THOMASTON RURAL HERITAGE CENTER, Phase 2, 2004
Instructor: Andrew Freear
Abigail Billi Barnett, Melissa A. Harold, Paul E. Kardous,
Nathan D. Makemson, Robert B. White